Born and raised in the famous fishing port of Peterhead, Jimmy Buchan always wanted to be a skipper. He left school at sixteen to pursue his dream and, after serving a tough apprenticeship as a crew member for several years, finally bought his first boat in 1986. He called it the *Amity*, meaning 'friendship'.

As skipper of *Amity* and later *Amity II*, Jimmy would go on to enjoy thirty years' success at the sharp end of one of the most dangerous jobs in Britain. He has survived violent storms, misfortune and a declining industry to become a respected and successful skipper, and his frankness and sense of humour in the hit TV series *Trawlermen* won him many fans and fame.

The Chair and a board member of the Scottish Fishermen's Organisation, Port Convenor of Peterhead Port and a keen supporter of the Fishermen's Mission, Jimmy is a passionate voice on behalf of the industry. He lives with his wife Irene and their two daughters, Jenna and Amy.

TRAWLERMAN

JIMMY BUCHAN

sphere

SPHERE

First published in Great Britain in 2011 by Sphere

Copyright © 2011 Jimmy Buchan

A CIP catalogue record for this book
is available from the British Library.

ISBN 978-0-7515-4469-5

Typeset in Bembo by M Rules
Printed and bound in Great Britain by
Clays Ltd, St Ives plc

Sphere
An imprint of
Little, Brown Book Group
100 Victoria Embankment
London EC4Y 0DY

An Hachette UK Company
www.hachette.co.uk

www.littlebrown.co.uk

For Irene, Amy and Jenna

Acknowledgements

I would like to thank Geoff Philips, my relief skipper, and all the crews I have had the pleasure to work alongside in my career, good times and bad. Not forgetting all the skippers past and present with whom I've had the pleasure to trawl the North Sea.

My fish salesman Alan Mitchell, who has sold my fish for more than thirty years, and all the staff at the Don Fishing Company Peterhead, *Amity*'s agents.

Iain Smith, from the family firm of J. A. Smith & Sons, for the guidance and advice given to me when I was starting out as a novice skipper and vessel owner.

The BBC and Matt Bennett for making *Trawlermen* a true and honest reflection of life at sea onboard *Amity II*.

James Donn, Eric Smith and the late David Flett for the invaluable knowledge and experience that you shared with me in my early years as a skipper – advice that I still carry to this day.

And finally, thanks to all who contribute to keeping *Amity II* and her crew at sea safe year after year.

Contents

1

A LUMP OF WATER

The sky changed in the blink of an eye. One minute it was a crease of grey clouds. The next time I looked up, odd, unnatural colours blustered out across the horizon. Beside the narrow railings up and down the sides of the *Amity*, I could see a flock of gulls darting along the lip of the sea. They were shrieking and breaking the waves in a desperate last-ditch attempt to get themselves a supper, pecking at the guts leaving the side of the ship as my crew worked through the catch. The gulls below were wildly aggressive, fighting over the fish and diving for the innards as if their lives depended on it.

I have learned the hard way that Mother Nature has her own warning signals.

We bobbed along gently on board the *Amity* with a shallow

1

swell. The waters looked calm, but the sky and gulls told me a different story. The sea was a master of deceit. You had to trust your instincts and mine told me that a storm was brewing.

A hundred and fifty miles off the coast of Peterhead, there are moments when you feel a knot in your stomach and you suddenly realise just how vulnerable and lonely you are aboard your vessel. Like a little polystyrene bobble in a pan of boiling water, you are at the mercy of elements far stronger than you. There's no squirming out of a tight spot, when that spot – the sea – surrounds you. Slowly the reality hits home that no one else can help you now. Your fate is in the lap of God.

We were just three days into our trip. Poor hauls so far had scuppered our chances of turning back home early. An old skipper once told me, never let your crew go without a pay. I hadn't before, and I didn't intend to start now.

As a trawlerman you're aware that there are bad storms out there, lingering on the North Sea across the Viking, Forties, Cromarty and Forth regions. Storms and fishing go hand-in-hand, especially in the winter months. Three or four times across the winter, you'll get a rotten one. In the trade we call them 'deep depressions'. Deep barometric lows are measured in millibars and are illustrated by isobars that compact around them, increasing the wind velocity. In low-pressure systems such as those that exist above the surface of the North Sea, the winds generally rotate in an anti-clockwise direction, forcing the sea level to rise and producing stronger and stronger winds. The lower the depression the more violent the storm. A normal depression would deepen to around the 980, 978 level. The lowest I'd ever heard a depression getting was 940, 942. At that level, your ship may sustain damage for sure. That's the kind of weather that has seen boats go missing at sea. The kind of weather that takes men's lives.

That night the depression was being forecast to deepen to 950.

I knew the storm was coming even before the gulls flapped and the sky began spraying weird colours above our heads. The shipping forecast had given a general synopsis at 6 a.m. that morning and it didn't sound great. *Viking, Forties, Cromarty, south six to gale eight, increasing south-west seven to severe gale nine.* The barometer was falling rapidly at the west coastal stations. The 'falling rapidly' bit was a red flag. It meant that there was a good chance things would take a turn for the worse, but that was the chance that I, as the skipper, sometimes had to take. I have a saying about fishing: The risks are great, the stakes are high.

That day, they could not have been higher.

Weather systems generally run from west to east. They come over from America, gathering speed as they cross the Atlantic Ocean, depositing their miserable sheets of wind and rain over the UK before hitting the North Sea, where they burn themselves out. As a skipper, I don't care about the wind or the rain, or even the brewing. I'm only interested in the burning out bit. But I took the forecast with a pinch of salt. Sometimes the radio gave you bad information, and it happened that you went into the storm and it maybe wasn't quite as bad as you were expecting. I was a young skipper, eager to prove myself and totally fearless – or so I thought – and I figured that maybe that morning's weather update was a load of rot.

I had listened to the reciprocal forecasts to the west of the mainland as well – Bailey, Malin, Hebrides, the network of areas atop Ireland where Atlantic storm currents fester and gather, ready to launch themselves across Britain and detonate on the north-eastern coast. My territory. It paid to look at the forecasts there, because that's where the weather would be hurtling in from, and along this volatile band, the news was also gloomy. Fishing vessels in the western areas were thinking the same as me, right now my only concern was the *Amity* and her crew.

At half past midnight each night, there would be an additional real-time, actual weather update. This was a skipper's one and only chance to get a true picture of the North Sea, rather than relying on forecasts. Lighthouses stationed around the British Isles would feed you the actual weather states – wind force and direction, as well as the barometer pressure reading. After a day of surreal skies and manic seagulls I was waiting anxiously for the nightly report. I listened hard at 12.35 on the dot as the live update came over.

Viking, Forties, Cromarty, north-westerly storm, force eleven.

My worst fears were being realised. Force eleven is one step away from a hurricane. The report was terrible news; force ten storms have the potential to claim lives at sea. A real bad one was coming at us. We were in for a rough ride, no doubt about it.

Up in the wheelhouse my eyes were glued to the barometer. I'd been checking the thing every hour, giving it a wee tap, could see the pressure dropping. That barometer was my only indicator as to the storm's pressure. There was no TV or satellite aboard the first *Amity*; I was totally reliant on my limited experience, which told me to keep an eye on the barometer and listen to the shipping forecasts. I was my own meteorologist, looking at the wind direction, listening to the forecasts, trying to work out what course of action I should take. The lives of my men depended on it.

Nowadays weather forecasting is very advanced. The *Amity II* has half a dozen computers, satellite GPS, you name it. Twenty-four-hour weather charts can give a skipper a blow-by-blow account of a storm as it intensifies. But back in the 1980s, the equipment was cruder. I had to make a decision virtually blind. It was something that preyed on your mind when you were fishing during the unforgiving winter season. If the storms sounded bad and you were heading out, maybe you'd stick to fishing close to the Shetland Isles. Lerwick port was within easy reach if the weather turned nasty.

Lerwick wasn't an option for us. We were too far out now. A hundred and fifty miles, and the storm was at force nine at the Shetlands and force eight at Aberdeen. Nowhere to turn. I weighed it up in my mind, and I'd be lying if I didn't at least halfway regret the decision to stay out to fish that extra day in the first place. Despite the outlook we'd put on a brave face and remained at sea, hoping to make a catch. Of course, I was scared of the impending bad weather, but on the other hand your business mind was telling you that if the weather wasn't so great, fewer boats would be out at sea. Fewer boats meant less catch being landed at the pier, and less catch meant I'd get a better price at market and make a bigger pay for the crew. I remember looking at the barometer all the time and hoping the depression hadn't deepened. Then the forecast came on and confirmed the outlook. They could have saved their breath and just used one word.

Terrible.

When you break it down, being a skipper is all about calculated risks. After three days and fifteen slack hauls, the seas had calmed and the whitefish catches were starting to look good. A promising catch earlier in the day with plenty of cod and haddock, and the decision to stay out longer felt like the right call to make. More of the same would go a long way towards filling the four hundred-odd boxes sitting below deck, waiting to be piled high with fresh fish.

The storm picked up.

We'd pushed our luck. And pushed – it seemed – a little too far.

Lerwick was a hundred miles away. Peterhead was a further fifty miles, or eight hours' steaming, but I'd rather brave the extra miles and return home than waste time sheltering in Lerwick, away from my family.

The blotchy sky quickly gave way to a pitch-black night. There was no depth or shape to the darkness, it was absolute. Even when the sky is filled with clouds you can usually spot the moon shining weakly through, as if it were behind a drawn curtain. Not this night. It's creepy out there, I thought as I gazed out through the window. Peaceful and quiet. Skippers don't like quiet seas. You can't trust them.

My neck muscles tensed up. I knew what was happening.

Calm before the storm.

When a deep depression comes in a skipper has two courses of action. If he's close to port, he can cut his losses and run. The danger is that if you're steaming through the water at eight knots over turbulent seas, you run the risk of a big impact and the resultant force of tonnes of salt water smashing into a two-hundred-tonne boat. It's not been unknown for boats to lose entire deck shelters when the waves smack down against them.

Or the skipper can choose to stay put and dodge. Now, to perform a dodge, you have to point the vessel's bow facing the wind and put the boat at a speed slightly faster than dead slow. Sometimes you won't even be moving through the water. Just bobbing on the surface. The only thing the skipper is looking to do is keep his boat pointing into the wind and swell to try and make it more comfortable on board. The act of dodging helps to control the level of roll and pitch that the ship suffers from in a storm, so any waves that come crashing in have less chance of damaging the boat.

That's the theory, anyway. In reality, it doesn't always work out that way.

I found myself in a proper rock-and-a-hard-place situation. Part of me was eager to try and bide our time in the storm – for twelve, twenty-four hours, whatever it took – and then get on with making a few more hauls. The other part desperately wanted to get away from the bad news and make for the safety of the harbour.

A hundred and fifty miles. I weighed it up again. The storm sounded too violent and I didn't fancy two or even three long days of clinging on for dear life as the boat rocked back and forth along the waves like an empty crisp packet. What a lot of people don't appreciate is that being in a storm is utterly exhausting – physically as well as mentally. You cannot sleep. You're being tossed about in your bed, and your body tries to compensate for the constant rocking, muscles fighting to keep you in the bunk even as your eyes are clamped shut. All you've to look forward to is a restless night's fitful sleep. At the end of it you wake up with your body sore and aching from head to toe.

Dodging is a test of endurance. If the skipper decides to dodge, he and his crew need to brace themselves for a long and bumpy ride. On one of the first boats I worked on, we had to dodge for three long, wretched days. Throw in two days' worth of fishing beforehand and by the time the storm passed we were knackered, and it wasn't even time to go home yet as the fishing still needed to be done. That trip lasted six days in total and I don't think, hand on heart, I'd ever been more exhausted in my entire life. When I got back home from that trip, I couldn't even remember getting into my bed, I was that dog tired.

No, I told myself. I wasn't going to sit this one out. It would have to be a cut and run job.

I increased the engine speed. *Amity* was now making good speed through the water, six, maybe seven knots as we headed towards home as quickly as we could. But fast as we were, the storm was faster and we were heading straight into it. As we raced back west the calm quickly evaporated and at the same time the winds swiftly picked up, an eerie whistling sound cracking through the clouds that suddenly exploded into a full-blown roar as the next few hours passed.

The waves swelled, charged with energy from the coming storm and forming what we call broken waters, big curved waves several metres high that folded over and turned in on themselves. The *Amity* was starting to dive and rise into the growing surf as its energy increased. A vicious jet of sea spray hit the wheelhouse windows with a deafening crash, like a million grains of grit striking the glass. I could hear the wind howling in the rigging and the ominous rumble of the sea as *Amity* headed in a homeward direction. It wouldn't be long before the broken waters would be bearing down on us. My gut wrenched at the prospect. I tried not to think about it.

There was no time to waste. I called out to Johnny, the first mate. He approached the wheelhouse door and leaned in.

'Tell the lads to stow her up!' I shouted above the racket.

'Aye,' Johnny barked back. No more needed to be said. He saw the look in my eyes. Normally I'm able to hide any concerns I might have, but on this night, my worry was visible on my face like a lighthouse beacon. He knew we were going to get a hammering.

The crew knew the drill. They were good boys, sharp and honest – they didn't need to be told twice. They battened down the hatches and lashed the nets, making sure that nothing could get washed overboard. The storm doors also needed to be shut. In a matter of minutes everything that could come loose on deck or inside the ship had been tied down.

Storms are very unpredictable but the one thing you are absolutely guaranteed is that it is going to be a bumpy and uncomfortable ride, and everyone on board knew it.

All the guys hunkered down in the galley, reading books or flicking through old magazines, or just having a bit of a blether, anything to get their minds off the impending storm. We were as prepared as we could be. The rest would be up to our old friend and sometimes foe, Fate.

Back in the wheelhouse, I saw the thing I'd dreaded.

A big lump of water, heading our way.

In the trade, lumps of water are powerful rogue waves out of pattern with the rest of the sea. They charge fast across the surface, crashing against the boat. The worst thing about a lump of water is that you can see it coming, even in the dead of night. You know it's going to hit and you're powerless to do anything about it. No choice but to sit tight and let nature run its course, sick to the core of your stomach with the knowledge that big rogue waves can tear your boat into shreds.

The lump was maybe five metres tall and four waves away, hurtling towards us like a giant rollercoaster car. The edges of the rogue wave were brilliant white, glinting like cold steel. The hairs on the back of my neck stood up. This thing looked absolutely ferocious. I steeled myself in the wheelhouse and stopped the boat dead. It was important to get the weight off the *Amity*. If you've got a two-hundred-tonne ship being hit by a four-hundred-tonne wave, the last thing you want to do is add any more energy to the force of impact. Cutting out the engine would reduce the speed of collision between the boat and the wave, making the wave less violent. But only by a fraction.

When you stripped away the ifs and buts and possiblys, being on the *Amity* was still going to be like standing on the epicentre of a scale-eight earthquake. I braced myself for the inevitable battering.

In a flash the big lump of water was on top of us. It slammed into the side and sent the whole boat into a powerful shudder.

Imagine the worst turbulence on an aeroplane, multiply it by ten and you still wouldn't come close to the violence caused by a lump. The wheelhouse windows flashed dramatic white as tonnes of water smashed against them, like a million paparazzi clicking their cameras around my ship, blinding me.

As the lump passed over the white foam drained away. The decks were flooded. I could hear water cascading off the top of the wheelhouse roof, sounding like the rush of a nearby waterfall.

My heart pumped quickly. This could be it, I told myself. Boats get lost at sea. Good men have gone out, never to return. By and large, there are no problems. We're seasoned men in a hard job and we get on without complaint. But sometimes there is a problem, and you don't come back.

The wave had passed over and we were still hanging in there. I breathed a sigh of relief and went down to the galley to check on the crew. No one was there. I went below into the cabin and could see the crew hunched up in their beds in the dimly lit, narrow space, smoking cigarettes in deadly silence. Caffeine and nicotine kept the adrenalin flowing. Two of the guys were buried in novels, taking their mind off the rattle and roar gripping the vessel. I often think that fishermen make good book readers, with so much time on their hands and little else to do during a storm. Others lay on their bunks, hands resting beneath their heads as pillows, eyes wide open and lost in thought.

No one slept.

The cabin area was a raggedy mess, like a bomb had hit the place. Magazines, newspapers and clothes were strewn over the floor. With the storm hatches shut, there had been no fresh air below deck for several hours and the atmosphere was so clammy it stuck to my clothes, wrapped me like a blanket. An acrid smell of diesel fuel, fish and saltwater clung to my nostrils. I told the boys not to worry, stay tight, and with a wee bit of luck we'd be out of the storm and back in Peterhead soon.

'Aathing's gaun to be okay,' I promised them.

'Aye,' they responded in unison.

I wasn't sure if they believed me.

I fixed myself a cup of tea and went back up to the wheelhouse. My trusty old sea legs ensured that I didn't spill a drop as I struggled to get up the nearly vertical stairwell. I had my mug in one hand, hanging on to the rails with the other. Then I made another quick check on the barometer.

The glass was at murder; the barometer was now even lower than before. A few hours passed, the storm reaching its peak, and yet outside the skies suddenly turned calm and quiet. There was absolutely no wind for an hour. No wind, but the sea continued to rage. From all directions tremendous waters came at us. I was pushing the *Amity* to the limit. Her engine and propeller groaned, working overtime as we bobbed westwards.

I knew the calm didn't signify the end of the storm. Far from it. Energy scampered through the waters like an electric current. That, combined with the very low barometer, could mean only one thing.

We were in the eye of the storm.

And very soon, conditions would be ferocious.

I looked at our location on the chart. Back then, with no satellite navigation system, pinpointing our exact position was often time-consuming and extremely difficult. By my calculations we'd made good distance since the storm had taken hold and now sat eighty miles from harbour. Eighty miles from the comfort of our homes and our own beds.

I maintained the *Amity* at full speed. Told myself that this weather window would not last. Two hours of eerie calm followed, as the eye of the storm hovered over the boat. I counted every mile we drew nearer to Peterhead, still hoping we might not get the forecast weather, but it was more wishful thinking than real expectation.

A short while later, the wind picked up again. Bang, just like that we were right in the thick of the action. Within seconds, forty-knot winds came roaring in from the north-west. The next few hours were going to be absolute misery. I'd have to slow the *Amity* right down. After all, she was a wooden boat and if we raced at speed and hit a huge sea, she'd burst right open, gutted like the fish I'd handled below deck in the days before I became a skipper. A split like that would prove catastrophic.

The hours passed as the rains lashed down and the winds bellowed. I peered out of the drenched wheelhouse windows and saw another lump coming straight for us on our starboard side. This one was massive, more than ten metres high, and just thirty metres away and three waves back. She looked like a tenement building. I had no time to do anything except say my prayers. People wonder why fishermen have a strong religious tradition. I'll tell you, this is exactly why. At sea you realise there are powerful forces in the world, forces beyond your control. The only one who can help you is your Maker.

I hoped the lump would miss us.

Amity was a twenty-year-old wooden trawler. She was a faithful boat and hadn't let me down once in our relationship – for it is a relationship between skipper and boat. She did, though, lack the steel strength and resistance of the more modern ships. Never had I been more intensely aware of the boat's construction than at that moment. I realised that all that kept the *Amity* watertight was a bunch of nails and caulking.

Wooden vessels are much more susceptible to damage than steel ships, because the rails are at risk of collapsing if the sea crashes into the side of the boat. On a wooden boat the hull is held together by a series of planks called ribs lying across the hull. They stop abruptly at deck level, where a further set of ribs called rails are bolted on to the existing ones, connecting them across the length of the boat. If the rails become damaged, water gushes in, torrents of the stuff. At the time it was not unheard of for boats to have their entire top rail smashed in. Others had the shelters on their decks completely ripped off and washed away with one awesome wave.

In the worst case scenario, the seams that ran between the sides of the hull and the deck could smash, flooding the engine room and the fish hold, causing disaster. The boat would sink in the time it took to make a cup of tea.

Two waves back now. The lump roared and widened, like a dinosaur opening its mouth.

I braced myself for the impact.

Johnny had joined me in the wheelhouse seconds before. One wave away.

'This is the Big One,' I said.

I slowed the *Amity* right down just moments before we were about to be swamped.

Here it comes.

A white-hot brightness blinded us as the second lump of water struck against the side of the boat, a flash of lightning striking the hull. I clung on to the ship's wheel and felt the *Amity* keel right over, the force so strong that I could sense my bones shaking with the ferocity of the impact. I was scared. I'd been at sea hundreds of times, thousands even, but not in all my career had I encountered a storm as violent as this one.

The *Amity* rocked. I couldn't hold on any longer, the force rippled through the wheelhouse, flinging me against the far wall, my back banging into the hard wood. A tide of charts, empty tea mugs and anything else that was loose rained down on me.

That's when the realisation struck.

She was near on her beam ends.

The beam ends are the struts that tie the ribs on the side of the ship. When a ship is on its beam ends – that's a skipper's worst nightmare. It means the vessel is rocking back and forth like a pendulum, being forced over on to its side.

We lurched sideways like a loose surfboard on the waves, the whole world tilting. The boat made strange groaning noises as she tried to cope with the pressure of the lump beating down on her. The intense, scary noise of the sea deafened me. So much energy swirling about in the water, the sea threatening to do some serious damage.

My heart lodged in my throat. I couldn't breathe; I was more terrified than I'd ever been. When survivors talk about their life being in the balance, this is what they mean.

All this is happening in a matter of seconds; but it seems so slow, like a dream. The moments stretch out, as your fear reaches new heights.

The ship started to roll back in the other direction. My heartbeat accelerated with joy. She was coming back up. Tonnes of water fluted along the deck as the *Amity* righted herself. I felt a huge sense of relief surge through my body, we had made it. Johnny stood silent, lost in thought. Slowly I brought the *Amity*'s engine back up to dodging speed. I fixed another tea and lit up my fortieth cigarette of the day. My hands were shaking so badly I could barely hold the cigarette, let alone smoke it.

Still seventy miles from home now, I took the decision to give up trying to outrun the storm. Mother Nature had won on this occasion. It was time to bed down and dodge. I looked at my watch. Two o'clock in the morning. I made it eighteen hours since I had managed to catch a bit of kip.

We began to dodge. Then I left the wheelhouse and joined the rest of the crew down in the cramped galley area, leaving Johnny on watch. The last big lump had put the wind up the crew as they were all up in the galley blethering nervously about it.

One of the lads yelped in pain; he'd scalded himself with boiling water while trying to pour himself a cup of tea. The lower half of his arm blazed scarlet, but despite the pain, the lads gave him a bit of banter to try and make light of it. A ghostly mist swirled in the air, the legacy of a hundred nervously smoked cigarettes. Another lad ate a bowl of cornflakes. Every time the *Amity* yawed this way or that, he would delicately tip the bowl so the milk did not spill. Aside from bread, cereal is about the only thing that can be eaten safely in such hazardous seas. It's all right at first, but after days of nothing but wretched weather and cold Kellogg's, you start to crave a hot meal.

I crawled into my bunk down in the cabin and wondered how long the storm would take to pass. I hoped it would be less than three days.

Survival wasn't the only thing running through my mind. Why do I do this, I asked myself.

Sure, I could've followed the same route as my father, got a job ashore as an electrician or in another trade. Or gone to university like my brothers. Done a job where I didn't have to put my life on the line every time I went out the front door. Certainly a land job would've been easier on my wife and family.

When a fisherman is caught up in a grave storm, fears can play devilish tricks on his mind. The terrible thing about fishing tragedies is that the lost boat is rarely discovered after the fact, and so no one ever really knows what happened to the crew or how the ship went down. I've always believed that it's the result of a boat being so swamped by the sea that she is put on to her beam ends and doesn't have the momentum to come back up again. Just like the situation we had narrowly avoided.

I started to think about the boats I knew that had been lost at sea. There have been quite a few of them over the years. At least six in my lifetime alone. Communications were less well developed in the 1970s and 1980s, and it took a lot longer for information to reach people, sometimes two or three days before relatives knew the boat was missing. Search-and-rescue operations were then carried out, but forty-eight hours after the fact, everyone understood they were practically futile. In waters as cold as the North Sea, a man overboard would be dead within minutes, frozen to death long before he had time to drown.

I lay on the bunk and thought about one of those doomed boats for a while, unable to blot it out of my mind. The other crews in the fleet had presumed that she had gone turtle, which means a boat has been turned upside down. I remember asking myself over and over, What must it feel like, lying on your bunk and then the next thing you know, you're upside down, and the mattress is on top of you? You would know you were upside down, you'd feel it as the boat lurched sideways, throwing you into the side of your bunk, and suddenly you're on the roof.

That's got to be a terrible, absolutely awful feeling, because at that point the fisherman knows he's going to die, as the water cascades in through the hatch and fills up the cabin. Even if such a crew was lucky enough to be trapped inside an air bubble, getting out would be impossible. A boat is more familiar to a fisherman than his own home, but now it would be utterly alien to him. I'd like to think that in that situation, a crewman just has a heart attack or passes out. It has to be better than going down with the ship and suffering an agonising, drawn-out death, the chill waters stinging your skin, pushing you back into a corner from which there's no light, no warmth, no escape.

No matter how good your boat is, if your time is up, your time is up.

This terrifying thought kept rolling around my head. In the end I gave myself a slap and forced my mind to focus on being optimistic. If we had survived that last wave, I thought, somehow we'd get through the rest of the night.

It's not my time. *I'm not ready to go yet.*

The lads were having a cup of tea. It never ceases to amaze me the conditions under which a seaman can put on a brew. I had a cuppa and a cigarette. Adrenalin shots. I was suddenly very hungry and realised I hadn't had a cooked meal in more than eighteen hours. Mouldy bread slid back and forth on the galley table, as I searched in vain for a slice that was mould-free. I settled on a slice peppered with green bits and greedily attacked it. It wasn't exactly dinner at the

Dorchester Grill, but my weak tea and mouldy bread tasted brilliant.

I climbed up the narrow, small-stepped staircase that led from the galley into the wheelhouse for an anxious glance at the barometer. Relief swelled up inside me: the pressure was rising rapidly as the end of the storm passed over us. The back of a deep depression is inevitably worse than its front, because the anti-clockwise direction means its pressure builds up and then releases energy at the end of its cycle. With the screamer gone and the pressure rising, they were all the signs I needed that we'd survived the worst. For the first time in many hours, I started to think beyond the storm. My spirits lifted a wee bit. I began to feel frustrated about the time we'd wasted at sea, how we'd been at the mercy of bad weather. Business sense quickly takes over from a fisherman's fear of drowning. A skipper is only as good as his last trip, and I didn't want to lose more valuable time.

At six o'clock that evening, the new forecast came in. Nearly a whole day had passed and I still hadn't slept a wink. The backs of my eyes were sore, my mouth dry as a desert. I was tired, hungry and my legs were stiff as frozen mud, but the forecast immediately cheered me up.

Force nine to eleven, decreasing to six to eight.

The words were like music to my ears. They told me that the worst was indeed over. Conditions still weren't going to be easy – not with all that energy that the sea had absorbed from the storm over the prevailing day and night, and only a marginal decrease in the wind strength, but it felt like a victory all the same. The *Amity* had come through the other end in one piece. We might not have had a full catch, but I was still happy.

I also took a moment to put in a message across the radio to my wife. In those days, the only way of letting Irene know I was okay was on a one-way radio speaker. Irene could hear me, but she could not talk back. Each day while I was at sea, I would get on the radio at six o'clock in the evening on the dot and chatter away into the set. I didn't know if anyone was even listening at the other end. Each message would start with me whistling a specific tune. That was the signal to Irene and the bairns that Dad was about to talk. Irene would fetch Jenna and Amy and sit them in front of the speaker while I spoke about how my day had gone. I'd say I missed them all very much and would be home soon.

I didn't mention the storm and left out the bit about the *Amity* being on her beam ends. The less they knew about that particular story, the better.

Finally, the storm burnt itself out. No time to celebrate, I told myself. Just get back to the job you originally came to this strange place to do: fishing. My attitude, and that of the crew, was that yesterday was a storm day; today a fishing day. We were still sixty miles out and over some good fishing grounds which had served me well in the past. I decided to wait until dawn before we shot our nets. The crewmen were shattered beyond belief, even the young guys hobbling about as if they'd completed a marathon, red-eyed and nerves shredded. But they were eager to get on with the work, because everyone was desperate for a good pay. If we went home now, they'd be left with barely enough to feed their families. Nae fish, nae pay, as the saying goes.

There was no rest. Sore arms and legs got straight back to work. Nobody complained, nobody gave up. This is the life we've chosen, and we have to make the best of it. We got the show on the road.

The rotten weather skulked on throughout the day and at gone six that evening, the storm had not yet completely cleared. What felt like a mild storm to us would probably feel like being spun about inside of a tornado to landlubbers. But given half a chance, I will always try and get the nets out to make a haul. If a skipper's not hauling then he's not earning money. Whenever there's an opportunity to get your gear on the ground, get shot and start towing, you do it. After all, that's what you're there for. A fisherman isn't really a fisherman, you see; he's actually a hunter and a businessman. And it's vital to his business that he never forgets this fact.

As the day continued, the weather relented and the sun began to creep out from behind the tar-grey clouds that lay low over the North Sea. In the space of twelve hours we went from being fed up and jumpy in the teeth of a vicious storm, to hauling in a big catch of premium-quality whitefish. That's the way it is at sea. Your fortunes can turn dramatically – and it pays to be brave.

Johnny and the lads were down on the deck gutting the latest catch. It'd been a bumper one, and the pained expressions of yesterday had given way to wide grins and a lot of the banter, talk of dreaming about cod and haddock that night, what they'd spend their pay on when they ran ashore. I put a brew on for them. Making the crew a bit of tea was the least I could do to show my appreciation for how well they'd coped with the appalling pressure.

Shunting tiredness to the back of our minds, we worked throughout the night and into the early morning, sorting the catch and shooting the gear again. I don't know why, but often the catch after a storm is a good one. It must be something to do with the energy charge in the sea; makes the fish go erratic, throwing great big shoals into the comfort of Jimmy Buchan's nets.

Johnny smoked a cigarette on the stern and I joined him. His ganzie – what we call a thick woolly jumper – was drenched through. I could've smelled the sea salt and fish oil coming off him, if I didn't stink of the stuff myself. He looked up as the last of the stars burnt themselves out against a sleepy dawn. Sometimes the beauty of the sea is staggering. On the one hand it wields this terrifying destructive force. But on the other, it's a place of mystery and wonderment. One day I'd like to go below the surface and see what it looks like down there – what secrets the North Sea is hiding.

We took in a further day's fishing, another good few hauls. With the fishrooms packed to capacity, it was time for me to give the crew the good news: we were setting a course for home.

The *Amity* returned to Peterhead early the following morning. The weather was overcast, a dirty grey film suspended over the town. There are probably better pictures to put on a postcard than a wet and drizzly Peterhead, but coming into the port mouth that morning it looked to me like the most beautiful sight in the world. To the northwest I saw Rattray Head lighthouse, located some six miles north of Peterhead. To my southwest stood the Buchanness lighthouse in nearby Boddam, a couple of miles down the A90.

Of the two lighthouses, Buchanness is closer to home and boy, was I glad to see it that morning. It's not much to look at – at least, not from the shore. A simple red-and-white striped tower fixed to the end of a low, jutting edge of coastline, surrounded by meadow grass and brown-grey rocks. But at sea, as you come into port, you see it flashing, long before you've sighted land, and your heart skips a beat, or maybe two. On a bonnie night you see it fifteen miles away, and soon as you do, you start to think, Aye, we're coming home tonight.

Lying in between was Peterhead harbour. The breakwaters, the pier, the beach and the outline of the town traced in the background. As we entered the harbour mouth, I realised that a large number of boats were docked up. Skippers had, for the most part, decided against taking a run in the foul weather. Not me.

The market pier was empty. Usually it's a bustle of activity inside that room as fish agents and wholesalers haggle over price and quality of catch, workers in wellington boots dragging boxes of fish towards the back of lorries waiting to ship the fish south, to Edinburgh and Glasgow, Manchester and London and abroad to France, Spain and beyond. That morning, ours were practically the only boxes, and the agent's voice echoed in the hollow room.

We had three hundred and fifty boxes' worth and unloaded them into the fish market in a couple of hours. I usually looked forward to watching my sales agent get a good price for me at market. But on that morning I left him to it. There were only a few boats to land a catch, so the auction prices were going to be big. Besides, the only thing I wanted to do was get everything in order, clean up the boat and return home to Irene and my bairns Jenna and Amy. It was only when I stepped on to dry land that it hit me just how much I had missed them. You try to block out such thoughts when you're at sea, because you have to focus fully on the here and now, if you're to stay alive.

Experiencing a really bad storm was awful, but it made you appreciate your family and how much you loved them. I was knackered and stank of diesel fuel and fish, my throat was dry from furiously chained cigarettes smoked in the hour of tension, and my bones throbbed. Scars of the storm. When I got home, though, I mustered up some energy and gave my daughters big hugs. They held their noses and made a face as I rubbed my unshaven face against their cheeks, the beginnings of a sea beard. Yes, all right, Dad smelled. I was so glad to see them I could have cried.

Risks were great. Stakes were high.

2

THE BLUE TOON

It takes a special type of person to want to become a skipper. You have to have grit, determination and a single-minded attitude to life. There are times when even the best fisherman starts to have doubts about whether a life at sea is for him, but the secret to succeeding is to push those doubts to the back of your mind and get on with the job at hand. If you're prepared to put in the hard work, you will reap the benefits.

It was a lesson that had been drummed into me ever since I was a wee boy, growing up in the town of Peterhead.

The town is known to the locals as the 'Blue Toon', and the people as 'Blue Tooners'. How this came about nobody is quite sure, although it might be due to the fact that Peterhead folk are also called 'Bloomogganner'. 'Moggans' were blue worsted stockings that fishermen traditionally wore, along with a 'ganzie' – a knitted blue jumper. This sort of unofficial uniform was designed in order that, if a man's body was discovered at sea, the colour of his moggans and ganzie would instantly identify him as a Peterhead man, and he could be appropriately repatriated.

Peterhead's a unique place. I was born at a time when its fishing industry was in the doldrums. I came from humble beginnings. The third of four boys, I was the only one who had his heart set on a life at sea. My oldest brother David, along with Peter, who had two years on me, and my youngest brother Kenneth, all had different goals in life to me. Kenneth, for example, was a great junior golfer and a Scottish boys' champion when he was fifteen. While I always had my eyes on the fishing, he was totally hooked on golf. He ended up going to America to do a golf scholarship and liked it so much he settled there. He works as an accountant but still has an excellent handicap and plays off scratch or plus one.

Peter, though, was my mentor. Some of my fondest childhood memories are of Pete teaching me how to make a homemade kite using nothing more than some bamboo, a sheet of brown parcel paper, a roll of string and a glue made out of water and flour. That was my early education in engineering, although the first flight of each kite inevitably ended in disaster and a return trip to the kitchen table for modifications. Years later, we'd be sharing engineering work of a different kind when Pete became an electrician and serviced repairs to the *Amity* when she was in port.

At the time I was born, my father played a very important role for a local factory, a textile mill. This factory supplies some of the world's top designers, including the likes of Stella McCartney, with bespoke fabrics, continuing a tradition of skills handed down from generation to generation.

This was just as electrics came into use. Prior to that time, the mill machines had been powered by water or steam. Now the factories came equipped with the latest electric looms and, if any component failed, it had to be fixed quickly. Time is money. My father had the responsibility for the equipment and for ensuring the mill ran a smooth operation.

The attraction for my father was that, in the old days, accommodation came with the job, on site. A good thing for the mill, as their electrician was never very far away. This was where I was born, within the boundaries of that building. My father, like myself, had aspirations and, with three young boys to look after, he decided to start his own business, even though by doing so he lost his accommodation. He must have been living under tremendous strain, going self-employed and having to find a home for his young family. Long ago, most families in Peterhead had limited means; they lived frugally in rented accommodation or had council homes. Only the wealthy actually bought their own houses, and for my father to decide to buy, well – that was a huge gamble.

We moved into what's called a but-and-ben.

Scotland has some fairly uncommon building styles: the bothys and black houses of the Highlands and the town steeples and mercat crosses familiar across the country. But-and-bens are Peterhead's contribution to that tradition, and part and parcel of our way of life. They're small, granite, two-roomed houses built for the fishermen. I reckon fishermen must have been on the short side back then, because the door-ways on most but-and-bens barely reach five feet in height.

The ground floor is split into a small bedroom on one side of the house and a small living room/kitchen area on the other side, with a slanted attic on top used for storing fishing nets. The loo is outside. Our attic had been converted to bedrooms, what with my mum and dad having three and then four chil-dren to care for. The bedroom walls were covered in wallpaper featuring racing cars – Jim Clark and Jackie Stewart were the heroes of the day.

Our beds stood in the middle of the room, because when you went to the sides the ceiling sloped at a sharp angle, forc-ing adults and even wee boys to crouch. A single staircase, steep enough to pass as a ladder, rose up into the attic, the only way up or down. Me and Peter would jump from the attic with-out our feet touching a rung, sliding to the bottom, our hands smoking. For us brothers, living in the attic felt like a *Boy's Own* adventure, a real kid's dream, although it got mighty cold in the winter months as there was little or no heating up there. And in the summers it'd turn stifling hot.

To begin with, we were three boys living there, as there was a gap of six years between my birth and Kenneth's – years in which I got all the rewards of being the bairn of the family. Kenneth was actually born Kenneth William Buchan. As soon as we brothers learned that we'd soon have another boy to add to our group, we had our hearts set on naming him Bill, so my parents gave him the middle name William. The four of us now lived in that attic space, though never felt cramped. The limited space meant we had to share beds, but no one ever complained, partly because that's all we'd ever known growing up. And partly because we had such happy times in our childhood.

Over the years my father gradually added more extensions to the but-and-ben, until eventually he'd transformed it from a small two-room house into a lovely home – a living room, four bedrooms and a fine kitchen for my mother to cook in. Unfortunately, by this time he no longer needed all this space: his four sons had all become men, left home and got married.

My family came from an area to the north of Peterhead which was once a separate village called Buchanhaven, with its own pier and local fishermen. Inevitably there were a lot of Buchans in the area, and a lot of J. Buchans at that: Jimmys and Jakes and Johns and Jameses. In order to avoid confusion about which particular Buchan you were referring to, your family name usually had what's known as a by-name that harked back to previous generations. My grandfather's by-name was Black Jock – I presume down to his dark skin tones, because we've got Spanish ancestry in our family – so my father, whose first name was Jim, would've been known as Black Jock's Jim.

People would say to me as a lad, 'Who're ye, boy?'

'My grandad's Black Jock,' I'd reply, burning red with pride.

Immediately they would understand which Buchan family tree I belonged to. If I told someone I was James Buchan, I could've been *any* James Buchan, and there's more than a few of us around Peterhead, believe me! By-names and the like might sound a little strange, but it's the only way people could easily identify who you were. Another family of Buchans had the by-name of the Oxys. Someone would see this person across the street and say, 'That's John Buchan over there.'

'What John Buchan?'

'Oxy's.'

And you'd know which family they came from.

Taking on my grandad's by-name gave me a connection to my past, and I figured he must have been highly regarded and popular: the older people in town all spoke very well of him. The tradition of by-names continues to this day, to a certain extent, although the influx of people from other communities to Peterhead has provided us with a wider set of surnames. But the fleet, for example, had many J. Buchans, so we had to have by-names in order to differentiate between one set of Buchans and another. One John Buchan, a skipper, was known as 'O.V.' after his boat, the *Ocean Venture*.

Even first names weren't set in stone in our town. My father always referred to me as 'James'; to my mother, I was 'Jake'; and to my wife today, I'm 'Jimmy'. I'm not sure how these different versions of my name sprang to life, but I respond to all graciously.

The richness of Peterhead culture went beyond names: we had our own language in our neck of the woods. The Doric is the local tongue, regional to mid-northern Scotland, and is one of many colourful languages in this part of the country, drawing its influences from Old Norse and Old Germanic.

I'm led to believe that the term 'Doric' comes from a reference to the Dorian people of Ancient Greece, who were said to live in rural areas and spoke in their own distinctive voice. Since Edinburgh was known as the 'Athens of the North', Doric was the name given to the language of the people from the more rural areas of Scotland. Scots Doric, for sure, goes back several centuries, and has become as embedded in the local culture as the fishing. I've known people from Peterhead to go on big cruise ships and meet Australians and Americans who find that they can only understand every third word coming out of their mouth, and that's when they're making an effort to talk 'proper' English. If I'm talking to someone in Doric, an outsider might not understand even that many words!

The Doric is as rich and diverse as any language you'll hear. Ears, for example, are called lugs. 'My lugs are sare' means 'My ears are sore.' 'It's gay caul nicht,' means 'It's very cold tonight.' 'Fit' means 'what', 'adee' means 'wrong', and 'louns an quines' means 'boys and girls'. It's a unique and wonderful tongue, and something which binds us all together in a special way up in

Peterhead and north-east Scotland. The Doric even has its own festival: 'A twa wikk lang splore o the tung, sangs, music and traditions o oor byous Doric culture.'

Other words are pronounced differently. We say 'mak' instead of 'make' and 'he-id' instead of 'head'. When you hear a person talking Doric in full flow, it sounds utterly unlike the English translation, and it's one reason the fishermen didn't object when the BBC added subtitles to the documentary series *Trawlermen*, about the lives of myself and my fellow fishermen in the Peterhead and neighbouring fleets. I think my fellow skipper James West put it best when he said he can't understand some of the types of Doric spoken in Caithness, Moray or even other parts of Aberdeenshire. If we struggle with it, then it's only natural that people further south would need a bit of help.

I was always conscious that I had to make myself understood when I got involved in the BBC TV series, but catch me having a chit-chat with a local fellow and most people would be hard-pressed to follow the conversation. It's what we've been brought up with – or, to put it in Doric, 'Fit wye bin bracht up wi.'

Language wasn't the only unique part of our community. Burnhaven, a small village to the south of Peterhead, was home to Scotland's first convict prison, visible to the south of the harbour across Peterhead Bay. Before the prison, known officially as HMP Peterhead, was built in 1888, Scottish convicts had to be sent down to English jails to do their time. Along with the building of the prison, a state-owned railway line was constructed, allowing passengers to travel all the way down to Aberdeen, thirty miles to the south. Sadly the line closed a long time ago.

In the days when prison labour was still allowed, the convicts helped to build the south breakwater to create a harbour of refuge, using local Peterhead granite. Breakwaters protect the harbour and surrounding coast from the weather, and the project was an essential part of developing Peterhead port. It took some seventy years for the breakwater to be completed, but it's something that fishermen have been grateful for ever since.

Hard work was drummed into me from an early age. My father grafted long, hard hours as a self-employed electrician. He loved his job, so much so that he retired not once, not twice, but three times before he finally rested his tools for good aged seventy-five. He was an extremely hard-working guy; I think I got my work ethic from him. He was known as a workaholic and worked six days a week, taking only Sundays off, clocking on at eight o'clock in the morning and not finishing until nine or ten o'clock at night.

He came from a background where you were taught that, as long as you had work, every other problem in life would sort itself out. His desire to work hard meant that, although he worked from home, us children didn't see him except in passing, when he was on his way out to pick up materials for a new job. He had a family to feed and provide for, and his determination to make a success of this focused his mind on the task at hand.

Our mother was a permanent fixture in the kitchen. She served up food morning, noon and night. She was a disciplinarian, making sure we went to bed on time, and she rarely had to tell us to do something more than once. If she spoke twice, boy, was that your last chance. I never heard my mother tell us boys to do something a third time; the tone of her voice said it all.

Life was fantastic for us. Sure, there wasn't a lot of money. Then again, no one had money. In our life people were divided up into the poor and the *really* poor. A few rich folk lived up the road and had careers as doctors and lawyers; instead, we had camaraderie and a sense of freedom. We had to make our own entertainment. As young boys we'd get out and get up to all sorts of mischief in and about town.

The but-and-bens were quite narrow houses and were built next to each other, with little space in between. We'd tie a piece of string from the handle of one front door all the way to the neighbour's front door opposite, leaving six inches of slack on one side. Then we'd knock on both doors at the same time. The slack tightened as one occupier opened his door, then as the second guy opened his door he pulled the first door closed, this going on until the penny dropped they'd been set up!

Other times we'd play a game called the Tapper. This game was better suited to night time. We'd stick a tack into the frame of a window on a house, and attach a line of thin thread to it. Then we'd wrap the thread around a nut, drag the length of thread over the garden and across the street, and hole up behind a dyke so we were out of sight. We'd pull the thread, making it tense and forcing the nut to tap-tap-tap against the window. The incessant noise was guaranteed to rile the owner. Do it enough times and the guy would hit boiling point and come out the front door, torch in hand, to scour the area for the Tapper culprits. We'd pull really hard on the thread, forcing the tack and nut to come loose, retrieve it in a jiffy and then scatter.

Rumbling the spoots was probably my favourite game. Long ago, spoots, or drainpipes, were made from cast iron. We'd find an old spoot and shove a screwed-up newspaper into one end and light it with a match. The whole spoot rumbled as the air filled with soot and it sounded as if a rocket was about to launch from Cape Canaveral.

I'd say we got up to mischief rather than we were outright naughty. And although our games were no doubt annoying to the people in their homes, I think it's an important part of growing up as a lad. We had a properly boyish upbringing, and all the better for it. Boys will be boys.

No boy our age was complete without his catapult. These weren't bought in a shop, however; our catapults were hand-made and we had to venture into the woods to find the exact type of tree to be able to make the crutch. When we laid eyes on a good specimen, we'd climb up the tree to cut off the right

'V'. Then it was off to the saddler to get a leather strip for the sling and a pouch for the stones we used as ammunition. Every little boy in Peterhead had a catapult stuffed in his back pocket, making his way down to Buchanhaven to set up some old tin cans on the rocks down at the beach and practise his shooting skills for hours on end.

I knew my parents were there for me if ever I needed advice, but I give them credit because they never steered or interfered with my life. Of course, they did their bit as we grew up, but they made it clear that we had to plan the path we wanted to take in our lives in adulthood. Thankfully for me, I'd known since a young age *exactly* what I wanted to be when I grew up.

The fishing heritage of Peterhead was ingrained in my bones from an early age. The town harbour was the focal point of the day's activity with the oldest part of it, Port Henry, dating back to the 1500s. The oldest building in Peterhead was the old smoke-house down by the River Ugie, which flows into the North Sea just a five-minute walk from Buchanhaven. The smoke-house was built way back in 1585; to this day, smoke can be seen pumping out of its chimney.

Then there's Fisher Jessie, a statue located along the cob-blestone pavements of the town centre, where she can still be seen to this day. A plaque explains that Jessie is a fisherman's wife, and the statue shows her hauling a wicker basket on her back, brimming with herring. Creel wives, as they were called at the time, carried their baskets up and down

Peterhead and the surrounding area in the first half of the twentieth century.

One of my favourite places to visit as a kid was the local museum, the Arbuthnot, one of the oldest of its type in Aberdeenshire. There was a treasure of relics to be found there, preserved from the days when Peterhead was one of the prime whaling ports in the world, and I'd be down there constantly as a kid, checking out the stuffed Arctic animals and Inuit artefacts. These objects spoke of a world far removed from the town, of somewhere magical and unknown. Even back then, the mystery of the sea fascinated me.

Throughout the nineteenth century, the men of Peterhead would set out on the North Sea in search of whales and their sought-after blubber and oil, on trips lasting five or six gruelling months as they sailed towards the Arctic Circle. Their expeditions took them as far afield as Greenland and up to the Davis Strait, all the way around to Inuit territory in Northern Canada. It gets fairly brisk in Peterhead during the winters, but I can only imagine how bitingly cold it must have been for those men, the glacial winds lashing them, their hands and feet frozen to the point where they actually felt like they were on fire.

The whaling men in those days weren't just tough as old boots; they were the best sailors in the world. When Sir John Franklin went missing trying to find the Northwest Passage in the Canadian Arctic, his wife, Lady Franklin, lobbied the British Parliament and managed to get a search party organised, with a £10,000 reward for finding the expedition. It was Peterhead men who went looking for Franklin, but sadly he wasn't found alive: the entire expedition had starved or frozen to death.

Some great figures have made their mark on Peterhead down the years, men who have single-handedly shaped the fortunes of the town, and when I was a kid people would regale me with stories of heroes from bygone times. Of all my idols, the Gray family were top of the list: David Gray, his son John Gray, and John's sons David, John junior and Alexander. They were gentry who, more than anyone else, made the town what it is today by establishing themselves as the first Scottish owners of whaling boats. Up until that point, the boats had been manned by Englishmen, but the owners supplying men from the other end of the country and transporting them north, found themselves unable to turn a profit. It was suggested one day that, there being an abundance of hard-grafting, God-fearing men in Peterhead, they might be well-suited to the whaling.

David Gray senior got his own ship, the *Perseverance*, and his family went on to make huge profits from whaling for the next hundred years. David and his son and grandsons were legendary captains who transformed Peterhead from a sleepy, isolated Aberdeenshire coastal town into the biggest whaling port in Britain, as Peterhead men set sail for the Arctic in search of twenty-metre-long, one-hundred-tonne whales.

Tragedy hit their family when John Gray the elder died. But that didn't stop the family from taking to the seas. Their will to hunt the whales could not be broken.

I was fascinated by the hard, gruelling lives of those Peterhead men, and listened eagerly to the stories of how they mastered the capture of these huge creatures. I take a risk whenever I go out to sea, but those guys were in much greater peril. Once they'd spotted a whale, they'd give chase to it, rowing for mile upon mile in the small whale boats. The men stepped into these flimsy structures knowing there was a fair chance they'd die.

They would approach the whale, edging closer, until the tip of the boat was very nearly bumping against the whale. At that point the harpoonist would spear the whale with his weapon. The most hair-raising moment was yet to come, however, because the harpoon caused the whale to go into shock and attempt to pull away while the crew hung on for dear life. The whale thrashed about with its fins and head, creating an almighty splash, and the men on the boat well knew that if the whale rose out of the water, it'd flip them into the freezing Arctic Ocean, where they'd die in a matter of minutes. There was nothing they could do but cling on for dear life.

The danger to the men wasn't over yet. The wounded whale would dive beneath the surface to escape the harpoons, and the crew had to jettison plenty of rope over the side of the boat. If the rope attached to the whale snagged or snapped, they'd be dragged underwater. The actual killing of the whale took some time, up to half an hour.

Like the fishing industries that succeeded it, the whaling was tremendously profitable for a while. Blubber was rendered into whale oil, which was then used for street lights, leather, cosmetics and soap. Victorian women used baleen, or whalebone, in corsets.

What stood out for me, however, wasn't the danger of catching the whales or the harsh living conditions these men had to put up with. It was the financial risks the owners took to fund these long expeditions up to Greenland. Whaling ships cost a pretty penny, and there was no guarantee that the ships would bring back a profit to cover the owner's outlay. But the rewards when the ships did catch a whale and return to port were massive: a single trip could earn a vessel more than half a million pounds in today's money. There were fortunes to be made, but you had to be a brave man, and a gambler – and you had to have luck on your side too.

Whaling is out of fashion these days – and with good reason. Numbers have declined, whale oil is of little use and several species are endangered. Countries which have a whaling tradition, such as Iceland, Greenland and the Faroe Islands, make the bulk of their money through whale meat. But whaling is the first example I encountered of the hunter instinct of the fishermen. Guys in a boat, hundreds of miles from home, in treacherous waters, seeking to slay a creature the size of a lorry – it's a remarkable picture.

The whaling drew to a close in the last years of the nineteenth century. Steam boats were coming into fashion and few of the whalers could afford the conversion to steam power. The saying of that day was that, when the Grays stopped sailing, the whaling would die. John Gray junior died in 1892, and the following year the great captain David Gray came out of retirement one last time to lead a crew aboard the *Windward*. After he returned to port in August 1893, David retired, dying of gout three years later. It was the end of an era.

The herring trade was developing, and it made no sense for these giant ships to go hunting whale when smaller boats could travel nearer to port and collect a profitable catch. I reckon the crews not having to be so far away from home for months on end had something to do with it too.

When the whaling died out, herring suddenly became the lucrative catch. At the beginning of the twentieth century, hundreds of steam herring drifters sailed out of Peterhead to go hunting, setting a pattern for the next hundred years: fishing boom and bust.

Still, growing up in Peterhead, us kids really felt as if we were part of a community. Everybody knew everybody in our town. Today, Peterhead's changed and we get our fair share of newcomers to the area. Back then, the fisher folk knew every face in Peterhead.

As a boy, me and my friends would play down at Buchanhaven pier, a granite structure that fed out into the wide expanse of the North Sea, flanked by a narrow beach pitted with stones and layers of pungent seaweed. Buchanhaven pier might not have looked the grandest pier in the world, but for Peterhead kids, the place was the site of endless adventure. Directly beyond the pier towards the village lay a road connected to the brae, where we children would race on a hurdy-gurdy, a self-made vehicle. You went and found an old pram somewhere, dismantled the pram and took the wheels, got a plank and a fish box and made it into the ultimate bespoke vehicle. We would race them down the brae, steering them hard left or hard right onto the pavement.

One day, one of our gang, a boy called Steve who was about three years older than all the rest of us, built a super-duper hurdy-gurdy with a big plank. About ten of us piled on, and when we raced down the road there was so much weight on the hurdy-gurdy that we couldn't turn, and we ran straight off the brae – the slope of the hill – into mid-air and crashed into the wet sands.

It was at Buchanhaven that I first learned about the thrill of catching fish.

My first experience of the sea came at the age of nine, on a small creel yawl my father owned down at Buchanhaven. Yawls were small craft that were originally developed as lifeboats to commercial fishing vessels and were adapted to become basic fishing boats. You'd set the lobster pots, known as creels, along the coastline a couple of miles out, load them with bait – usually offal and off-cuts from the fish processing factories – and put them down to let them soak overnight. Then you'd pull them up the next day, hoping to get some brown crabs or lobsters that you could sell on at the local fish market.

The yawl belonging to my father was about twelve feet

long. It was a sort of hobby of his, and he'd take us out to haul the creels on summer evenings after work had ended. I loved going out with him and when I was a child, the adventure out to the coastline was the highlight of the summer holidays. The oldest of us siblings, David, wasn't so keen on the trips, and as for Peter, he'd always turn green with seasickness the moment the yawl abandoned dry land. I, on the other hand, loved the sense of freedom upon leaving shore, the exhilarating thrill of being a hunter.

Seeing the lobster, the ultimate bounty, as the creels were hauled up, was an exciting moment for a nine-year-old lad, this black-clawed creature trapped inside the pot, just waiting to be turned into someone's dinner.

We kept our catch in a submerged holding box a few hundred yards up from Buchanhaven pier. The reason for the distance between the holding box and the pier was that fishermen are, by nature, guarded and protective of their catch and, should the other yawl men see how many lobsters we'd reeled in, they'd be armed with vital information about the number of lobsters on a particular area of coast. Our technique was to return to the creels after dark and make sure our backs were turned shore side when we put our catch in the holding box. That way, the fishermen on the quay side discussing the issues of the day couldn't see our bounty, although the more time we spent loading the box, the more suspicious they'd become that we were on to a prime spot.

For a few days in the summer, the whole place would smell

awful. The bait was left in a bait box beside the yawls for days on end, and the stench was so foul that it began to attract rats; they would hide in the bait box, a concrete box three feet square with a wooden lid. The bait box was a good source of food for the rats, and I can remember well the day a creel man was going to the box for bait prior to heading out in his yawl. As he lifted open the lid, a number of rats rushed out of the box at high speed and one crawled up his trouser leg. As he was jumping about on one leg doing a poor attempt at a Highland fling, we were making up the brae as fast as our legs could carry us. To this day I still have a phobia about rodents.

Adding to the smell were the broken-off lumps of seaweed that the storms dumped along the craggy coastline. There were thick great clumps of it that would build up, like piles of dung. When the sun came out the old seaweed would start to rot, and if it was hot enough it would create a stink so overwhelming you had to fight your gag reflex. On those rare but unpleasant days, you'd be praying for the seaweed to disappear. The next day your prayers were answered as a big tide came in and washed the whole lot away. Locals said the decomposed seaweed made great compost; I never really had the desire to handle the stuff, so I wouldn't know about that.

My father eventually sold his yawl, but that didn't stop me getting some valuable fishing experience. As a young, energetic boy of ten, I'd turn up early in the morning and wait for the chance to head out with someone on their yawl. If my luck was in, there'd be space for me. Otherwise I'd come back and

try again the next morning. My hunger for the work probably helped me secure a trip out: because everyone knew
everyone else in Buchanhaven, all the yawl owners were highly
familiar with my face. When I came back from one trip I'd ask
the next creel fisherman what time he was going out tomorrow morning. If he said seven o'clock, I'd be there at ten to
seven, waiting eagerly for my next chance at sea. As we were
just kids, we didn't get paid for it – I was only doing it for the
thrill and to get a bit of inside knowledge about fishing. I'd pay
great attention to what the creel men were doing, observing
them closely. The skippers were mostly older salts, retired
seamen, but they would still be in touch with what was happening down at the main port. At every chance I got, I'd listen
in to their conversations.

'Big Pat's come in with a big shot from the Bergen,' one of
them would say. 'Aye,' another would say, remarking that it was
all cod fish. The Bergen bank was and still is a rich fishing
ground more than two hundred miles north-east of Peterhead.
Big Pat, or Peter Stephen to give him his full name, was one
of the top skippers operating out of Peterhead, and a cousin of
my father's, and I would hear a tale nearly every week about
the huge catches he brought home from the North Sea. The
locals seemed in awe of his feats. It only whetted my appetite
further to get out there myself. It was psyching me up for life
as a fisherman.

The pier was my playground, all day, every day, throughout
the summer. Even when I was just five or six years old and too

small to be working on the yawls, I would be down at the rock pools with my rusty tin can, looking for crabs or making a little boat out of pieces of wood lying about and floating it in the pools. It was here that I felt truly at home.

I can remember playing down by the rotting seaweed and the rock pools and seeing the bigger trawlers going back and forth out of the main port at Peterhead. They looked absolutely gigantic, fishing vessels of all shapes and sizes. I would watch them set sail one day and recognise the same ones coming back a few days later, their fishrooms overflowing with whitefish. Even back then I knew, deep down, that one day I was going to go out there myself and do the same job. I felt, in my own wee way, that I was destined for it.

3

THE HUNTER INSTINCT

By the age of twelve I had my heart set on being a skipper. I had an obsession with the sea. Just to look at it from Buchanhaven pier made my spine tingle, and on the short trips out for lobster, I got a huge buzz from making a catch. Equally I knew there was money to be made in the fishing trade. Seeing how hard my father slogged while having to make do with limited means strengthened my desire to follow a different route. Like my father, I was prepared to put in the hours – but I wanted a high reward in return.

I was also inspired by tales of my grandfather, the afore-mentioned Black Jock. He'd been a fisherman from the Great Depression of the thirties all the way through to the fifties, when the industry was in a slump and the rewards on offer for a fisherman were meagre. In those days my grandfather would've come home from a season's fishing of six to eight weeks and had to 'pay in' – meaning he'd made a loss on the season's fishing and not turned a penny of profit for himself or the boat. He was so poor he had to come off the boat and go and do roadworks.

When grandfather went out on the boat in better times, the whole family got involved in the business. My aunts – my father's sisters – repaired the drift nets. These are nets with floats attached to the top and weights to the bottom. My grandfather was a herring fisherman, and to catch herring you had to shoot miles and miles of drift nets across the sea. Herring is a fish that lives close to the surface, preferring the warmer temperatures at shallow depths. Physically hauling in the nets required brute force.

They had a routine for the haul: one, two, three pulls and then a shake-shake to release the herring on deck, the crew repeating this ordeal for miles and miles of drift net. The bigger the catch, the harder it was to pull the nets in.

Fishing was very much a seasonal activity back then, and my grandfather's boat followed the herring as it moved around the British coastline. They'd go to Yarmouth and catch herring, and later in the season they'd set up shop at Scarborough. In the winter it was the west coast. For several weeks a year, everything needed for the business relocated to Yarmouth: the boats, the crew, the fish-gutters. This meant families moved down too; as well as fixing the drift nets, my aunts were gutters who used barrels of salt to preserve the herring before they were sent on to Russia, our main export market. The Russians loved their herring – cheap protein food for a poor nation.

Sadly I never really got to know my grandfather. He died when I was just three years old. My other grandfather worked at the woollen mill in Stornoway during the Depression. I'm led to believe that the mill in Peterhead, where he originally worked, also made Harris tweed. But a rule was introduced stipulating that Harris tweed could only be sold under that name if it was produced in the Outer Hebrides. When the factory relocated to Stornoway on the Isle of Lewis, my grandfather had no choice but to follow the work. These were hard times indeed.

My father regaled me with stories of Black Jock's life at sea, and that stoked my fascination. He told me how the herring boats returned to port after a night's hauling nets by hand, and how the catch was counted not in terms of boxes, or tonnage of weight, but using an obscure unit called a cran.

They stored the herring catch in woven baskets three-quarters of a metre deep. Three baskets equalled a single cran. If a boat came in and landed a hundred crans, the whole town knew that one lucky skipper and his crew had made a huge shot meaning a huge catch. The skippers benchmarked themselves against what the other boats were bringing home. Say you'd shot a hundred cran, the next guy caught eighty and the guy after that brought in sixty. You were the top dog, the number one skip, and for sure, your name would be the talk of the Blue Toon. Everyone in Peterhead would be discussing your catch in the pubs and shops.

According to my father, the information about the catch weight would be wired home to the Caley Group, which is, to this day, a fish-selling office based in Peterhead. His job, as a child in the after-school hours, was to head down to the Caley and read off the notice board which boats had landed what on that particular night. The locals called the notice board 'the billie'. Then he'd go home and tell his mother how his father had fared in the overnight herring fishery. That was how they knew where he stood in the skippers' league. Nowadays we have TV screens showing live computer updates of the landed catch, but the competition remains intense.

Not only did he go home and tell his mother the weight of the catch, he also knew the crew's wives. So he would also relay the information to them. There was always one woman who would tip him a penny or a halfpenny; and if he was lucky, someone would give him tuppence, especially if he told them about a big catch. I'm led to believe this was quite common at the time; you'd get all these boys on their bikes reporting the billies. The wife was always the first one to get the news.

For the longest time, there was precious little other industry in Peterhead to speak of, beyond the fishing. When the trade suffered, everybody in the town felt the pain. At the beginning of the fifties, things opened up a wee bit and non-fishing companies established factories in the town. I recall an American company named Cleveland Twist Drill had a local factory. Crosse & Blackwell originally came to Peterhead for the herring and switched to making Branston Pickle when the herring market dried up. On a Monday morning, you knew the factory was brewing up the famous mix. Their factory was situated up the road from the harbour, and the North Sea winds blew in an eye-watering smell of vinegar, mustard and garlic that hung in the air. Your clothes would reek of vinegar for days.

My grandfather didn't exactly earn millions as a fisherman but he was working at a time when the industry was in a slump. It was not uncommon for them to come in from a night's fishing, not be able to find a buyer for their herring and return to the sea to dump it. When I was a kid, the fishing was enjoying a good period. Besides, apart from the financial motivation, I saw how important the boats were to the community, and how the skipper was a glamorous figure, almost an idol among locals. Why, I thought, would a man want any other career when there was a berth on a boat, fish to be had and money to be earned?

With the heritage in my family, being a skipper was in my blood.

I attended the Peterhead Academy on Prince Street, only a few roads up from the harbour. However, I can't say I was the greatest student they ever had. I didn't get into trouble, but my mind was not perhaps as focused on my studies as it should have been. I treated school as a secondary activity. All my focus was on the day I would finally be able to go out to sea.

As I got older I would head down on my bike to the boat yard at the harbour to watch the new boats being built, two at a time. Back then, Peterhead was famous almost as much for building boats as for catching fish. After a severe depression lasting from the early fifties until the late sixties, there was a real buzz about the place again and I would see kids a few years older than me getting ready to go out to sea. On other days I'd wander down to the markets and look on as thousands upon thousands of boxes of cod and haddock were sold on to wholesalers for huge sums of money.

But the yard was where the action was to be found. My passion for being a fisherman was so great that at the ages of twelve and thirteen, I'd spend hours at the yard seeing these boats being built from the keel upwards in a never-ending conveyor belt. The guys launched one boat, and the very next day a new keel was laid for the next build. There were two- or three-year waiting lists for vessels, and as the fishing industry prospered in the late sixties and throughout the seventies, so the yard witnessed an explosion in boat-building.

Every boat that came out was bigger than the one prior. They went from being sixty-foot boats to lengths of around eighty feet. Twenty feet might not sound a big deal, but the boats were also wider, higher, deeper.

At this time most boats were built as dual-purpose trawlers, meaning they were designed for two modes of hunting, suited to two types of fish. One was for pursuing whitefish: cod and haddock. The other was to pair-trawl for herring. That way a skipper could adapt his vessel to the moods of the season, farming herring in the winter months and switching to whitefish in the summer.

I entered the trade too late for catching herring – by the time I had a berth, herring stocks were depleted and whitefish had become the main species to hunt – but I have it that it was a tremendous fishery because you had nothing to do with the catch: no gutting, no cleaning. Just straight into the fishroom and back to port as quickly as possible. Whitefish are bigger, and because the ripe grounds are generally found two hundred miles off coast you've got to gut the fish, wash it and store it below deck in ice boxes.

The race for herring meant that the more power your boat had to catch, the bigger an advantage you held over the other boats in the harbour. When it comes to boats, power is everything. Power permits a skipper to haul in ever bigger catches and that equals larger profits. A skipper was able to pay off a brand-new boat, at a cost of around £100,000, in a couple of years, whereas before it might've taken him ten or fifteen years to get the bank manager off his back. Once the old boat at three hundred horsepower was paid off, the skipper went back to the yard and commissioned a new vessel, only this one would have the capacity to operate at four hundred horsepower.

Government assistance also played its part in the boat boom. Skippers received a grant from the British government to help finance their boat, and once we joined the EEC, they were handed a European grant on top; twenty-five per cent of the total cost from each, meaning a skipper only needed to afford fifty per cent of the boat himself. This was back when the government worked with the fishing industry; I wonder now, will those days ever return?

Being around the yard and seeing these boats launched, I saw exactly how lucrative the business happened to be. It was hard work then, too, for a crew, but the trips were far shorter than I have to do on board the *Amity II*. They were out for a maximum of four to five days, not the gruelling ten-day journeys that we now have to do.

When a boat was in the stocks and taking shape, it'd get bigger and bigger until the last day before launch. Now the builders had to remove all the wedges that helped to keep the shape of the structure in place.

Word travelled quickly when a new build was ready to be launched. You'd hear of a day and a time, usually at the top o' the tide, when the tide is at its highest point, around two o'clock in the afternoon. Then, come the day of the launch, everybody in the town made their way to the harbour to watch this exciting sight. There'd be a naming ceremony to round things off before the ribbon was cut and the final wedges knocked out to allow her to slide down the slipway and into the water.

Once they'd been launched the boats remained docked in port for another three months, as there'd be plenty of work to be completed before a boat was ready to sail. Each day I'd pass the port and see some new addition to the boat: a whaleback being attached (this is a part of the forward deck which makes water taken over the bow shed down the sides of the ship), a wheelhouse being constructed, a mast or engine being fitted. Literally, I saw these magnificent vessels built from scratch.

As a boy I'd stroll into the yard with no health and safety officer to stop me. The yard seemed big and hollow as an aircraft hangar. The moment you entered, a strong smell of wood filled your nostrils, of the different timbers used to build the boats: oak for the ribs, pine, larch, cedar. The smell of wood mixed with an overpowering and unmistakable stench of green creosote, a tar-based wood preservative. I'd hear the buzzing of fifty saws and the clunk of the hammers as shipwrights knocked in miles and miles of caulking – made from cotton and hemp fibres soaked in pine tar – inbetween the seams of the vessels. Tradesmen used to talk to me during their work; I'd know who was building the boat, know the skipper, and sometimes I'd see him down the yard, speaking to the shipwrights and seeing how everything was taking shape.

I made it my business to learn as much about each of these skippers as possible. With my dad based in an on-shore industry, I was aware, even at a young age, that I'd have to ask one of these guys for a berth one day, if I wanted any kind of career at sea. And berths were not at all easy to come by, not by a long shot, with all the money pouring in.

One of the skippers I looked up to at this time was David John Forman. His son was a friend of mine at school. Forman was a genuinely superb fisherman, and he built a boat called the *Resplendent*. Because his son was a friend of mine, I was granted special access to her. I saw that boat progress from a plan on the family kitchen table to the finished article and go on to become a highly successful boat. Forman always came across to me as a very stern man. I imagine, knowing what I know from experience, that he was a happy man in his own world. But to me, as a twelve-year-old boy, he seemed absolutely driven by success. David John Forman was one of the guys who showed me exactly what level of motivation I'd need to be a good skipper. His son, in fact, went on to become a top-class skipper in his own right. He went to the top, broke records, came ashore. Started a fish factory, built it up, sold up and moved on. An entrepreneur if ever there was one, and a sharp guy.

Other skippers inspired me too. Some of the herring men graduated from small boats and earned enough money to afford massive pelagic ships built in Stavanger, Norway (pelagic fish are herring, mackerel and other oily fishes, those that live closer to the surface of the water, as opposed to the species which live in deeper water towards the seabed such as cod and haddock). To me, these skippers were the shrewdest of the lot. They clearly anticipated the changing markets and were look-ing ahead to the next scene. Staying ahead of the game, not being afraid of change: as lessons went, this was an especially valuable one for me – and one I'd put into good use later in my career.

Looking back, I honestly feel the skippers of the early seventies had it a bit easier than I did. The sea was teeming with fish in those days, herring was readily available. The other side of the coin, I suppose they'd say, is that we've got the electronics, whereas they did everything by hand-drawn map. And they'd have a fair point.

A skipper in that day had to be a really sharp guy. He had to be a quick thinker, able to take what he saw in front of him and make sense of it in his head. Navigational skills were vital; everything was based on radio waves. Different radio waves came from different directions, so a good skipper would know which way to steam to get to the next fishing ground, without making any points on a chart, just by observing his on-board navigator and interpreting the radio waves from the transmitters. That's a real skill and one, I imagine, it takes a long, long time to master. Nowadays I've got several computers on the *Amity II*, and if I want to go to a certain point on a map, I select it, switch the boat to autopilot and away we go.

Much more electronics, the old skippers say.

Fish biting one another's tails off, and government grants to ease the burden, I reply.

Things just change, I guess.

Tucked away two miles west of Peterhead is Inverugie – the place where the doctors, solicitors and businessmen lived in the grandest homes in the town. The River Ugie would meander through this affluent area. This is where I'd go fly-fishing for salmon in the summers as a teenage boy. In the morning I'd rise early and bike the few miles to the river's edge, where I would watch the regular fly fishermen, armed with my rod, fly and a flask filled with hot tea. Finding a spot, I'd perch myself at the edge for the entire day, trying to catch fish. I wasn't a very accomplished fly-fisher, but I enjoyed pitting my wits against these evasive salmon. Older people lined the banks and were on hand to give me advice: it's too early to fish, the sun's too bright, the water's too shallow, my fake fly's not deep enough in the river. I'd listen and absorb everything, trying to improve my chances of hooking a salmon.

When I finally managed to get a bite, it felt as if I had Moby Dick himself tugging on the end of the line. The salmon fought like mad, jerking the line this way and that, and I struggled to keep hold of the rod, my whole body pounding with excitement. I was also tactical about the salmon: I'd get a catch and return to the same spot the next day, eager to repeat my success. Sadly, I never set the world alight when it came to fly-fishing – but it did awaken the hunter instinct inside me.

When I turned fourteen I had the opportunity to catch salmon at sea, working with the local salmon fishermen. I fished with them in the summer holidays, clocking on at six o'clock in the morning. The routine was similar to the creel yawls, in that we'd sail to the salmon nets anchored two or three hundred metres off the beach, hoping to see a good catch from the previous twenty-four hours. The suspense and excitement of waiting to see what rewards the sea held added to the excitement as we pulled alongside the nets and peered beneath the crystal-clear surface. The older men clambered to the side of the boat.

I'd climb around, desperately angling for a look at the prize.

Their heads would lean over the edge, as if admiring their reflections, and then—

A roar!

Salmon swimming in circles in the nets, round and round. Big, beautiful salmon, still alive, thrashing about, their silvery scales glistening, the salty, fresh smell of the sea coming off them. These salmon weighed anything from ten to fifteen pounds – even more on some occasions. Sometimes there'd be one or two fish in the anchored nets; on other occasions we'd catch thirty. I say we, but I was only making up the numbers on the boat. Yet the catch made me feel like I'd snared the fish myself.

When we took them on board, the salmon were so lively we used to have to hit them with a stun; if we didn't, they had plenty of vigour about them to jump over the side and back into the water. The stun resembled a small wooden brush without any bristles. I'd bring it down onto the fish's head, battering the salmon till it stopped flapping about, by which time there was blood pouring out of its gills and splashing about on deck.

Back then salmon was known as a wealthy dish – a fish for the elite. Salmon was rare; nothing like the globally farmed fish of today. Once we'd caught the salmon we'd ice and pack them in special boxes, nailing the box lid down like a coffin. It was then a race across to the town of Fraserburgh – known as 'the Broch' and eighteen miles north-west from the Blue Toon – to catch the goods train on its way to London. The guy who had the salmon licence had some sort of a connection with London, and the deal was that any fish caught under him had to be shipped directly to the famous Billingsgate market in the south-east of the capital. I loved to think of our salmon journeying south, heading to the biggest fish market in the world.

In the hunter's world, I was beginning to see, there's little to top the joy of a good catch.

Along with the thrill of the fishing, I also caught my first glimpses of life at sea. The excitement of us deck hands was raw, but there was one person who generally avoided the celebrations of the rest of the crew, a man apart: the skipper.

He was a calm and serene man, the skip, known locally as Salmon Joe (his real name was Joseph Yule). He had the measure of his crew and led his men by example. No panic or nerves in his voice when the catch was disappointing; and no hysteria when nets returned a score of juicy salmon. The skipper, or 'mannie', behaved as if he'd seen it all before, and knew too much of the highs and lows of life to be moved. His voice was steady – or so it seemed. But I had a close eye on the skipper and saw that, every time the men roared, he allowed a little smirk to rise almost to the surface. The smile used to pop, like a bubble bursting, at the very last moment before it had a chance to spread across his face.

The hours on the salmon fishing boat were long, especially for a fourteen-year-old boy. The pay, however, was fantastic. I got £20 in my back pocket at the end of the week, while some of my friends doing paper rounds or being milk boys were on £4, maybe £6 with the tips loaded on top. In my eyes the gruelling hours weren't a problem – I was getting paid to do a job I loved, and paid grandly for the privilege. I was young, but I put a nail through every penny that I made aboard the salmon boat, saving nearly all of it, leaving me enough to buy a packet of ciggies. I didn't even know *what* I was saving for; I just thought that, having worked so hard for my money, and with such a big wage coming into my pocket, it made sense to keep it instead of splurging the lot.

Between the shifts on the salmon boat, I heard from friends a wee bit older than me about the jobs they'd secured in the fishing industry after leaving school. They'd left Peterhead Academy in 1974 and 1975, and everyone wanted a job at sea. Friends talked about the skills they learned, the hard graft and the huge catches, the new vessels being built down at the port and the modern technologies being used to make boats safer.

There was nothing else for it. As I entered my last year of school, I set my sights on a career in the fishing industry. I'd seen first-hand the pride and responsibility of the salmon skipper. Going out to the far reaches of the North Sea, I thought, was the thing for me.

Nothing would deter me from realising my dream.

The one regret I carry with me from these early years was

that I didn't try much harder at the Academy. At the time I felt that school had nothing to offer me and I showed only a passing interest in the classes. History has proven that having some academic qualifications in my pocket would've been of no hindrance to my career path. In my defence, the previous summers had given me a taste for sea work and I was desperate to get out on the North Sea and whet my appetite. When you have the itch, it can't be shaken.

There was money to be earned on those waves, and it could not be done at school.

If financial reward inspired me, however, I was also aware that I'd be entering a world where the risk of death and tragedy was all too real.

Back in the 1970s, it was quite common for a whole vessel to be lost at sea. Crewmen regularly died, getting washed overboard or dragged under by the nets. In the bad winters, however, the losses took on a different scale, and reports would reach our ears of a freak wave battering a boat and all hands being lost. The fleet lost around one ship a year. Sometimes more. Because we lived in a fairly small, tight-knit community, the loss of a crew affected everyone. The whole town was shattered. People were numbed. The loss of the *Trident* was one such tragedy.

The *Trident*, one of the prides of the Peterhead fleet, was on her way back from herring grounds along the west coast on a stormy night in 1974. Twelve miles off the Caithness coast at the Pentland Firth, a strait separating the Orkney Islands from the mainland, she suddenly disappeared, taking with her all seven crew members.

Nearly everyone in the town knew someone on board the *Trident* on that fateful night it went down. They were shocked and appalled at the loss of their friends and acquaintances. The whole community was saddened. Whenever you heard of a boat going down, you'd think to yourself, If it's bad for us, how must it be for the families of the men who went down with her? You're reminded of the fact that a mother is left to bring up the children and live with the legacy of such a terrible event. Many other families witnessed similar tragedies still too raw to mention. But despite the dangers, nothing could dampen my resolve to go to sea.

4

YOUNG LAD

At the age of sixteen, in July 1976, I was finally able to go out to sea.

One of the reasons I was drawn to the trade was the lucrative rewards on offer. Prior to me joining the party, in the late 1960s and early '70s, young boys heading to sea were able to buy a brand new car within two or three months of starting a fishing career. It was a bonanza in those days, you fished as much as you wanted and the men worked until they basically collapsed, and the whole town thrived on it. The future was bright and the money was good. I can remember being a wee boy and watching a brand new boat coming into Peterhead port. The first of a new style of steel vessel, she had cost the skipper something in the region of £70,000, which was a lot of money for a ship in those days. There were two old codgers standing next to me on the pier watching this brand new boat steam into Peterhead. As she was being tied up in the port following her delivery voyage, one of the old salts said to the other, 'He'll never see it paid.'

The other quickly replied, 'Aye, his grandchildren will still be paying for that lot!'

I would later get to know the skipper, Andrew Buchan, very well. He told me that the boat was fully paid for in just two years. And recently Andrew Buchan's sons have taken delivery of a brand new vessel that has probably cost about twenty-five times the price of their father's original boat!

For a young lad dressed in hand-me-downs and brought up in a frugal family, it was eye-opening stuff. Hunger for a better life drove me on. The opportunities were there, if you were prepared to grab them.

As much as money played a part, I was also drawn to the hunter-gatherer excitement of fishing. To me, that side of the business is what fishing is all about. You are connecting with man's deepest and most primal instincts. To put up with the storms, the seasickness and the twenty-hour days and sleepless nights, you need to be drawn to fishing for more than the money. You have to be motivated to pit your wits against Mother Nature.

My berth was to be on a boat called the *Responsive*. She was a big steel ship, and the skipper was a hard-working man called Joe Nicol. I already knew Joe through my cousin Emily, to whom he was married.

The *Responsive*, like a lot of boats at that time, was at the seine-net fishery, having originally been a purse seiner. Converting ships was often necessary in order for the skipper to move with the changing types of fishing activity. Seine net is a type of trawl fishing designed to catch cod, haddock and whiting as well as plaice and other species. Trawling is where your boat pulls a fish net through the water, scooping up your catch by reeling the nets in. In seine-net fishing, the fish are surrounded by warps laid out on the seabed in a triangular pattern with a trawl-shaped net at mid-length. As the towing cables, called warps, are hauled in, the fish are herded into the path of the net and caught. In contrast, purse seiners are pelagic ships, shooting their nets over a school of fish in a circular arrangement, closer to the surface. The net then closes up at the bottom, like a purse.

Seine-net fishing was known as a 'dark' fishery, because the prime catches came in the gloaming. In the winters we'd work in the days, and in the summers, by night. Sadly seine-net fishing itself went out of fashion in later years as the cod and haddock boom died out, with most of the fleet switching to trawling. Seine-net fishing made for a long, long day for the crew and required a high degree of skill to carry out, but if you got it right you'd produce a high-quality catch.

None of the crew of the *Responsive* called me Jimmy. Everyone knew me just as the 'young lad'. I was on what was known as a half-share. Boats operate on a share basis. Crewmen are not on a salary as they are self-employed, but rely on a share of the profit from the catch, the size of the share being determined by age and experience. This means all the crew are motivated to make as big and good quality a catch as possible, because if they don't, they will not get a pay. It's an incentive-based pay scheme. As the young lad I would only be getting half of a normal cut of the profit. That might not sound much, but as a sixteen-year-old with no experience, straight out of school, on a half-share I might expect to earn £200 or more from a single trip. Around the same time, my brother Peter was serving an apprenticeship as an electrician, for which he was paid just £40 a week. I was on big money.

I knew, however, that I would only progress to a full share once I had learned how to splice the seine-net rope, mend the fishing nets, and gut and wash the catch as well as how to be a good watch keeper. I had a couple of years' hard education in front of me yet before I could work my way up.

When I started out, if I'm honest, I was a useless article. The difference between being ashore and living out on sea was chalk and cheese and I struggled to cope with the transition. It was real hard work in a man's world, night and day, there was always work to be done. There was no such thing as bedtime aboard the *Responsive*. Let me tell you, my backside was booted a lot of times in those early days. But in the end, it was the making of me.

We would always set sail at half past midnight on a Sunday. Peterhead was a deeply religious community and Sunday was generally considered to be a day of rest, but although skippers accepted the Sabbath they were also keen to get out to sea for more catches, so they would leave as soon after the clock struck twelve on a Sunday night as was reasonable. This became known locally as the 'Back of Sunday' and turned into something of a tradition. Come midnight, women from all over the town would descend on Peterhead harbour to wave off their menfolk as the entire fleet, hundreds of boats, all poured out into the North Sea at the same time, fighting to get out first, bumping into each other in the crowded port waters. It was an epic sight, bustling and radiant. And I was proud to be part of that fleet going out to fish.

The situation is different these days. Whereas thirty years ago we'd set sail for six days, now we are going out for ten-day trips, with only one, perhaps two or three days between each voyage. It's a long time for a man to be away from his family, his friends and his loved ones, with no contact all that time. The demands on the modern-day skipper have meant that the Back of Sunday is no longer the tradition it once was.

Everything about life on board a boat was great – except I had to learn to cope with seasickness.

The sensation first hit me just after we had left the harbour mouth. The sea had a fair swell to it already, and the *Responsive* started to roll and pitch with each rise and fall of the waves. These were relatively gentle swells but I could not appreciate that at the time! Before we had left, the old salts had been warning me about the effects of seasickness.

'Fin it comes, ye'll be spewing until it turns green, boy,' they said.

Now I was feeling it. The smells on the boat – the thick, stale air, the taste of diesel always on my tongue – became too much, and just a few short hours into my first trip, I was running out from the galley up to the deck to vomit over the side. Weak and unable to stand upright, I shuffled meekly back down to the cabin and hunkered up in my bed. The world was spinning and I was suffering cold perspiration. I felt sleepy, and closed my eyes. The next time I woke up, an old salt was shouting at me to get myself out of bed.

'Come on!' he boomed. I looked at the clock. Several hours had passed, it was the crack of dawn and we had reached the ripe fishing grounds, so it was my job to go up on the deck and learn how to shoot the gear. The stuffy galley air had left my throat hoarse and I also needed to get some fresh air. The morning was sharp and crisp, a clear blue sky was dawning. But I was still struggling badly with the sickness. I went back into the galley to drink some water – even thinking about eating was enough to make me spew again! – and the smell of bacon and eggs cooking on the stove filled my nostrils. Here we go again.

I ran back on to the deck and leaned over the railings.

My skull thumped the entire time. I couldn't shake it, and with the added burden of the headache I found it impossible to keep up with the pace of the other men. It was non-stop, twenty-four hours a day. As the new half-share I had to stow

71

the ropes away as they were retrieved with each haul. We shot miles and miles of rope on to the seabed. Once the rope was shot, the skipper gave the order to heave the ropes back up, herding the fish circulating inside the confines of the net on to the boat. When the gear was being retrieved it would come around the winch on what's called a coiler, and we deck hands had to physically hold the ropes and stow them.

This was backbreaking work, no two ways about it. The ropes were heavy as bars of lead and as we were launching about eight or nine hauls a day, with each operation taking two hours. This proved to be a never-ending chore. It was men's work and I was but a boy.

You also had to be careful because you were working right next to an open winch. If the gear was uneven when the ropes were being pulled in, the skipper would shout at you to slacken one side or the other, known in the trade as 'surging' the ropes. Lots of men had been maimed or even killed in winching accidents. A hand or foot could get severed if it was wrapped around the winch drum, and there was even a case when a crewman was carried twice around the drum after his loose clothing became caught in the warp. You might think it unwise to put the novice lad on the most dangerous job, working within a few inches of equipment that would chew you up should you fall into it, yet in those days it was the norm for the new hand to get his hands dirty and put his body on the line.

Once I'd finished sorting out the ropes in between each

haul I would have to wash the fish from the latest catch and lower them down to the fishroom below deck using a basket. The pace was relentless and it was all I could do not to gag with each load of fish that I handled. The constant ebb and movement of the vessel left me feeling tired and depleted, and with the new workload I was having to endure, I often wondered, during those first fitful days at sea, if my future perhaps lay elsewhere than the fishing business.

I began every haul of every day at the beginning of a trip telling myself that I'd look for a new job the moment I landed at home. I didn't let these dark thoughts win out, though, and as the trips went by I got better at the work and, more importantly, the seasickness became tolerable. I was determined not to give up on my dream of becoming a skipper, no matter how many exhausting shifts I had to put in below deck. And besides, all my friends were fishermen and for me to give up – well, that'd make me a failure. In their eyes and mine.

There were a million other chores to get done too. Splicing the ropes was a mammoth task. As a seine net fishery we had miles upon miles of ropes, and if they broke then we needed to cut and chop and splice them back together again. This was a task that had to be done quickly.

Being able to maintain your gear and repair the nets was also an essential skill. Without working nets, the skipper couldn't make a haul, and he and the rest of the crew would be booting your backside in no time. Like a lot of the tasks aboard a boat, you cannot buy it, and you cannot learn it out of a book either. It was vitally important to watch the guy making the repairs and make a note of everything he was doing. I would be holding the net and trying to memorise what was going on. If I didn't hold it right, he'd give me a right clip round the lugs. It was hard to keep your mind focused at all times during the day, but if you were going to learn how to do it properly, you needed to pay proper attention.

Taking a watch was especially hard. You'd have to stand in the wheelhouse, in charge of the boat while everyone else slept or worked, including the skip. As a young half-share I would be sent on watch duty with the first mate. On the streets there's the Highway Code, and in the maritime industry there is what's known as the 'Rules of the Road'. These basically instruct you on the correct procedure for such things as passing and giving way to other vessels, always making sure you pass port-to-port, and if a vessel is giving you his port light, you give him your port light too. There are many hundreds of rules of the road, but in those early days I only needed to know the most basic ones. If you got into difficulty, there was always an experienced watch keeper with you to show you right from wrong.

And dare you fall asleep on watch – not the easiest thing to avoid when it's the middle of the night and you're sorely tired! The graveyard watch was the worst, two to four o'clock in the morning and only a constant supply of coffee and cigarettes for company – and pop songs, thanks to the magic of Radio Luxembourg, an English-language station broadcasting out of the Grand Duchy and the only channel that you could pick up at sea. Some lads were a bit sneaky and would try and wind the clock forwards by ten minutes to end their watch early. On one trip three lads on night watch all had the same idea, and when the skipper went up to the wheelhouse the following morning he was spitting mad, wanting to know who'd flogged the clock a half-hour forward. Needless to say, nowadays you've got Sky Plus, DVDs and iPods. It's a lot easier than it used to be.

Sleep was only to be had for a few hours at best, and when you slumped into your cabin bed, those precious hours passed in what seemed a matter of minutes. I'd wake up with my hands aching and covered in blisters from the harsh routine of stacking and stowing the seine-net ropes, the salt and sand rubbed into them like so much grit.

Life on the *Responsive* was a tough daily grind, and the other crewmen never allowed me to slack. Sometimes I was too slow at sending fish into the fishroom. Every ton of fish that was caught had to be lowered into the fishroom, basket by basket, by the young lad. In other words, me.

'We don't have all day,' they would shout up. Meanwhile up top I could hardly lift a basket of fish, far less lower hundreds of them into the fishroom to match the speed the crew were working below decks.

At other times they would tell the skipper that I didn't have the qualities necessary to be on the crew, with me standing not two feet away and in full earshot. When I look back, I realise they were just bringing out the man in me. That is one of the things that being on a fishery does. If there is a man inside of you, the sea will bring it out, make no mistake. We are fortunate to live in a world of luxury and plenty today, but it wasn't always so. To be a hunter-gatherer you have to put up with the worst that nature can throw at you. It's a painful process, but the misery of those early days prepared me for a lifetime on the ocean waves.

People are always amazed when I tell them, but I still suffer from seasickness to this day. Aye, it's not as rough as it used to be, but I do feel it, although only on the way out to sea. On the return trip I'm too happy to worry about it. It's one of those things that plays on your mind; if you're able to focus on other things, the effects soon pass.

When I began to cope with the seasickness, life on a boat had its own special energy. The buzz at sea with the crew was fantastic. There were a lot of young lads on board, they were all fired up and the banter was excellent. This sense of camaraderie kept us all going and enabled us to push ourselves to the limits. To give one example, you wouldn't dare admit to your crewmen that you were knackered. Saying you were dropping on your feet was like accepting defeat, so you would keep on going, otherwise the ribbing they would give you for being tired was going to last all trip. Sometimes your mind would be elsewhere, and the other lads would give you a poke and a kick. There was no motherly love out there. It was dog eat dog, and you had to deal with it or find a different job.

But it could be great fun too. Sure, the work was hard going, but you'd have a great laugh at sea as well. One time, there was a young lad called Stevie, he was seventeen, a year younger than us. Me and another lad by the name of Peter decided we'd try and put the fear of death into him while he was making a watch on the graveyard shift. We crawled out of bed at three o'clock in the morning and Peter pulled a white turtle-neck sweater over the top of his head. Then we snuck up on to the deck, to the rear of the wheelhouse. Stevie was sitting in the skipper's chair, listening to the radio and trying not to nod off. When we reached the back window I crouched down below it and started tapping on the glass and making wooing noises with Peter doing a good impression of a headless ghost. Poor old Stevie got the fright of his life. The look on his face as he turned around and saw Peter was one of pure horror.

Pranks were part of life on a boat. You'd always be looking to play a joke on the rest of the crew. One of my favourites was to fill another boy's gloves with grease or any other goo I could get my hands on. Then the next day you'd be missing your boots, and you knew that your buddy had gotten you back. The gags kept your spirits up. Out there you really had to look out for one another. If your buddy was struggling you'd be the first in there to help him, though you'd slag him off at the same time. There was hard work to be done, and you needed to stick together.

And because of the share system, every crewman knew that

he needed a bumper haul somewhere along the trip in order to get a good pay back at port. Everyone was pulling in the same direction and you were all hoping that by Wednesday night, having been out since just after midnight on Sunday, you would get what was known as a 'Homeward Bounder'. That meant that a skipper had caught a big shoal of fish, so large in fact that you did not have to fish the next day. You would be gutting all the way back to the harbour and spirits on board would be high. The advantage of seine-net fishing was that it was a highly effective way of catching cod and haddock. It wasn't uncommon to land four hundred boxes' worth of whitefish in a single haul. If this happened, we all knew we would be getting home a day early, and the money was going to be good. I was fired up working towards this goal.

After five long days at sea we were finally returning to port from my first trip. My initial reaction was, maybe I needed to consider a different career. I was absolutely shattered, had barely eaten or slept in a week, my face was covered in pimples from the lack of washing, as water was too precious in those days and was generally conserved for drinking. A tuft of hair was growing on my chin and cheeks. The skipper noticed and couldn't resist a dig. 'Is that belly button fluff growing on yir chin, boy?' he asked, grinning.

I wasn't finished yet. First the boxes filled with whitefish had to be lifted off the boat in a process called 'landing the catch'. Each box has to be grabbed and placed in the middle of the fishroom so the winch can lift it ashore. A single box fully loaded with fish and ice weighs around sixty kilos. I could barely lift my side of a box with another hand helping me, yet this same man was hauling boxes of fish weighing fifty kilos or more into the middle of the room all by himself. I couldn't believe what I was seeing. It was a stark reminder that I had a long, long way to go yet before I could prove myself worthy.

We usually returned to port on the Friday. Sometimes the catch wasn't great and we had to put in an extra day's fishing. On those occasions, instead of getting home Friday we returned on Saturday, but we still had to get out again Sunday night. But a short pit-stop was all we needed, a wee bit of time to recharge the batteries. Even though you were knackered from six days' fishing, you didn't get much rest ashore. At twenty-one years of age and getting in at seven or eight o'clock on a Saturday night, you'd be out on the streets in your glad-rags within the hour.

You were paid by noon on the day you returned to port, cash in hand. Suddenly you had a fistful of dollars and all the hard work seemed worth it. It wasn't unheard of in those days for some crewmen to come back from a trip and find a thousand quid in their hands. Twenty, thirty years ago, that was a lot of money. Some of the men would sadly burn their way through their notes quicker than they earned it, betting heavily in the bookies or spending the lot down at the bars on the drink. I was a little less frivolous; I would buy myself a new pair of jeans or a jacket for going out on the Saturday night, but I'd still put away the rest. In my mind, I was already committed to saving up for my own boat.

Once ashore from that first trip my view of fishing began to shift. Yes, the first few days had been rotten. But I had two days to myself and wouldn't be sailing again till the back of Sunday. I started to think, if I could keep at this for a couple of years and progress from a half-share to a full share, then I could get a chance to watch what the skipper was doing. A half-share would be too busy with jobs to observe, so getting to the full share was the immediate priority. But after that, a whole new world of opportunity might open up for me. Joe Nicol was a sound skipper and there were good men on that boat and I was willing to apply myself. I felt that I could learn a lot from them that would stand me in good stead when it came to launching my own boat.

I collapsed into my bed that first night back ashore, more tired than I had ever been in my young life. Every inch of my body was drained of energy. My body stank horribly of smoke and fish, I was unshaven and my hair was so thick with grease and salt that a comb would not go through it, but I couldn't even muster the strength to wash my face or brush my teeth. But as I lay on my bed, exhausted by my first trip fishing, I was comforted by the knowledge that I had coped with everything the sea had thrown at me. A little part of me was already aching to set sail again.

5

FRIGHT AT SEA

I liked working on the *Responsive*, but after six months I needed a change of scenery. My problem wasn't with the nature of the work – I felt like I was slowly coming to terms with the endless grind, although my sore limbs might have had something to say about that. But I yearned for a share on a more modern vessel.

Down at the shipyard a constant flow of new boats still made their way to the port, each one more technologically advanced than the last as skippers took advantage of the favourable budgets and grants available to get themselves a leg up over the competition. I knew, from watching these boats being launched, that the *Responsive* was a wee bit out-of-date, and that if I was to progress from my half-share to a full share,

I'd need to be aboard a boat that had newer features, so I could learn new skills. Newer vessels, for example, had rope bins fitted to the deck. These were essentially holes in the deck which allowed the gear to go right down into the hull of the vessel. Needless to say, this made life easier for a knackered deck hand. Some ships were even fitted with hydraulics, with rope reels which would wind the ropes in.

Meanwhile on the *Responsive*, we were still using the old-fashioned system of pulling in the ropes by hand. Truly this was the hardest job on board. Your muscles would ache and cramp up with all the effort of retrieving the gear, time was of the essence and you'd be dog tired from the hundred other chores needing to be done.

Hard work never killed anyone. So they say. But you have to grow into life on a boat, and boy does it take time. The growing is hard. When you go out for the first time, you're a puny little thing with not a scrap of muscle on your body. You've got no sea legs, so you're slipping about everywhere, having to hang on to rails all the time to stop yourself from falling about. I'd be holding a basket of fish, the boat would roll and both me and the basket would go flying. Sea legs didn't affect me just at sea, either. I'd land on the quay, take my first few steps back ashore and the quay would still be moving, swaying this way and that.

All the while, the seasickness has you in its grip; pounding away at your head, sending you into dizzy spells that make every task twice as difficult to complete, because it takes all your effort just to focus.

As well as my desire for a share, I felt things weren't really working out for me on the *Responsive*. Because of the age of the ship, bits and pieces were forever going wrong with her. We'd have to stop off at Lerwick to fix certain problems. On top of that, the *Responsive* went out for long periods – or so I thought at the time – with trips frequently lasting seven or eight days, spending the Sunday in Lerwick, and I was interested in a boat that'd be docked in the harbour of a weekend. The *Responsive* being Joe Nicol's first commitment, he wanted to go out for long trips in order to make ends meet, which was all well and good, but it killed my social life. For a lad of sixteen or seventeen in Peterhead, nothing much happened in the weekdays. Saturday night – that's when all the action was to be found.

When I did have the chance to go out with my friends, we talked shop, as most of them came from the fishing background like myself. We'd discuss the industry over a drink and, without realising it, be downright unsociable to others in our company if they weren't connected to the fishing. This was a bad habit and one I tended to avoid if possible. I've heard people say that fishermen talk of nothing else but the sea and their trade, and sometimes I think they're probably right.

At the beginning of 1977, I heard a berth had become available on another vessel, one that was a lot newer and offered me a bigger challenge. This boat's name was the *Fidelia*. I didn't know the crew. They all hailed from Fraserburgh, the big fishing town eighteen miles or so north of Peterhead. The boat, however, was registered locally. I got the number, called the skipper up and asked for the berth. My luck was in. I'd found a new boat.

I wasn't to know it at the time, but the *Fidelia* turned out to be the first vessel I'd take to sea as a skipper.

Several things attracted me to her. Unlike the *Responsive*, the *Fidelia* had been purpose-built for seine-net fishing. Put two boats side by side, and it's a sure thing that the one purpose-built for a fishery is the more efficient boat – and slightly more comfortable for its crew members. It had the rope bins already fitted, which made my work as a young lad much easier – and crucially, would allow me more time to learn the job of becoming a fisherman. I never dreamed of being able to skipper the *Fidelia*, but I thought, maybe if I get enough of an education here, I can progress up the ladder a wee bit. From day one, I decided to put in a hard shift on that boat, show my willingness to do the jobs asked of me, and see where that took me.

The *Fidelia* was a steel boat at a time when there were as many wood as there were steel vessels in the fleet, and was of a modern design: sleek, eighty feet in length, painted all-black with a 550 horsepower engine, a hugely powerful ship. And she'd never been designed with herring in mind, because at that time, the industry was undergoing a massive change. The herring died. The authorities and scientists blamed overfishing, with the result that, in the early seventies, a total ban on herring fishing in the North Sea came into effect. Until now, much of the Peterhead fleet had divided their trade between fishing for herring and whitefish. With the blanket herring ban, the fleet began to change. Some skippers focused more on the whitefish, while other vessels dedicated their efforts to following herring and mackerel around the UK coastline as the pelagic fishing grounds shifted with the different seasons.

To compensate those skippers hit hard by the ban, the government offered grant assistance for fleets to develop and pursue fisheries. Old boats were revamped and new builds were abundant. Literally, the boat yards couldn't keep up with the demand and skippers started going overseas for new builds.

The result was that the whitefish exploded: cod, haddock and whiting became the most valuable catches in the North Sea, and the newest vessels were being built with the whitefish market in mind, creating awesome seine-net monsters capable of landing vast catches. While half the fleet had to make do with adapted boats and coiler winches, the *Fidelia* had her nose out in front.

She was skippered by James Donn, a Fraserburgh man who proved something of an inspiration to me. We got on really well and from the moment I stepped on board, I knew I had a future on that boat.

Skipper Donn had a quiet air about him. I'd known a fair few skippers who thought it was part of their job to shout at their crews at the tops of their voices, but James was never like that. As long as we did the work to a good standard, he'd be okay, although he had the occasional off-day too, and these

times he'd boil over. I think that happens to the best of us –
and I speak having had a fair few bad days of my own!

I liked sailing with James. He was a steady earner and always
tried to get his crew back to port for the weekend. He understood that if a guy had even the back end of Saturday night to
himself on dry land, well, that was better than no return home
at all. I'd say that a day spent recharging his batteries sometimes
does wonders for a man's work ethic come Monday morning.
Today, of course, I take more time at home, but all skippers of
James's generation believed it was normal to fish just about
every week of the year.

James had many a story to tell of his early years at sea. He
came from a proud fishing family and working as a skipper was
in the guy's blood, and he always appeared keen to show me
the ropes. If I was trying to repair a hole in the nets, James
would be watching over me. That sounds stressful, but the fact
is, the best way to learn is to look at an experienced net
mender up close and copy him. Then he'd tell me to do a
small hole and if I got it wrong, I would be made to do it all
over again. James got me to hold the netting as he cut out the
hole to be repaired and showed the apprentice how it was
done properly. Sometimes I'd be knackered and let my mind
drift to another planet. He'd sense that I wasn't paying attention, and there'd be a wallop over the back of the hands with
the mending needle to wake me up.

My duties as a half-share still included tending the ropes as
they were retrieved from the seabed. I had to stand not half a

metre from a highly dangerous winch, the sleeve of my oilskin jacket dangling a few inches above, and were I to slip into it, the consequences would be fatal. I'd be looking at the handle we called the Dead Man. Pull on this and the winch would suddenly stop. Problem is, the handle was located smack in the centre of the winch, just about the worst place you could possibly put it. You'd have to lean directly over the winch to hit it, trying not to fall in yourself.

And we still had to wash the fish and lower the catch into the fishroom. Young boy's chores. But the winch allowed me to pick up a knife and learn how to gut fish. It might not sound like much, but believe me, this is a genuine skill, and it takes a long time to get it right.

When each catch landed on board, we'd scoop it by hand into wooden boxes stacked on deck and the six crewmen took up their stations. Three piles of boxes. Two crew to each pile. One man at either end of the box.

I'd pick up a fish, pressing my thumb lightly into the gill, knife in my other hand. Then slice in a downward motion, from the front of the fish all the way to the back along the underside of its body. On the return I'd jab the knife inside the fish, scraping out the guts as I carried the blade back up towards the head. Back and forth like that, smooth and quick. Whole operation took no more than a couple of seconds; at that speed, I had to be careful not to nick my fingers with the blade. If I didn't get the gut right and a bit of the liver remained, the mate would give me another clip around the ear. Gutting wasn't easy; the knife was blunt and you'd tear the belly and the mate was on your back.

Once the fish was gutted, it had to be washed and placed in baskets on the deck according to its size, the different sizes being different grades of catch. You wanted to get the washing done quick. You physically had to lift the basket of fish, pour it into a high-pressure jet washer to clean the fish, and then tip the catch back into the basket. The guts were tossed on to the deck floor, where three or four crew would cascade water on the deck, washing the foul innards overboard. The decks were drenched in water during the gutting operation; they were open decks, so we'd always get an ingress of water. On a bad day, there'd be so much water on the boat – cold, salty North Sea water – that it'd be squelching in our socks. Freezing our toes.

The baskets with the fish in them had to be stowed securely on deck prior to being lowered into the fishroom; you couldn't leave them standing about, not with the ship rocking back and forth. The man in the fishroom shouted out for a certain grade of fish. You'd get small, medium and large fish, but we had our own names for them: the smallest haddock were known as chippers (for the chip shop). Above them you got seed and pingers, and the biggest of all, the real monsters, were called chat haddock. On the cod side we'd have big ones, then sprag, followed by mediums, big-small and small, while the littlest ones of all were known as Robbies. Monkfish were also graded, with the smallest ones called banjos. I've not the faintest idea where the names come from, and crew never question them: the names were there when I was fifteen, and they're used now I'm fifty. One name does make sense, however – big prawns are called clunks, because when you take a large prawn and chuck it into a basket, it makes a clunking noise.

After my first few trips out, I started to enjoy the work in a way I'd never managed on the *Responsive*. For the first time, I looked forward to going out to sea. Hey, I'm getting the hang of this lark, I thought.

However, the sea had other ideas. I soon discovered that I could master a dozen different skills on the *Fidelia*, but the one thing the crew couldn't teach me was respect for the sea. That only comes when a lad experiences his first storm. And mine was waiting for me around the corner.

If a crew found they were too far from port at the weekend, with Sunday reserved for prayer and rest, the skipper would put in to Lerwick on the Saturday night and shelter there for the whole Sunday, leaving that evening. Some ships did fish on a Sunday, but by and large the fleet observed the Lord's Day. In the summer, if the weather was calm and the sea flat, we'd float along for the day, going swimming in the tepid water. To this day, some boats still respect that tradition.

On this particular occasion we were docked in Lerwick and Sunday was drawing to a close. James Donn was preparing for our cast-off in the early hours of Monday morning, when the skies were still coal-dark and the air cold as needles. A storm was brewing. The skipper took the forecast in the wheelhouse and the window happened to be open. I listened in as the detailed area forecast was transmitted over the radio. The crew always used to try and listen in, because the skipper never told you anything, so you gleaned what information you could by eavesdropping whenever the moment presented itself. We'd heard rumours among the other fishermen laid up at Lerwick that a bad storm was on its way, and the broadcast that reached my ears confirmed the worst of it:

Viking, Forties, the area of the North Sea we were imminently departing for, *North-westerly seven to severe gale nine, increasing to storm ten …*

With the forecast that bad, I was sure the skipper would cancel our trip. The rest of the crew agreed.

'Another night in Lerwick it is,' this old sea salt said. 'Aye, two nights' break in a row, you'll see.'

I suspect if the weather had been a one-off, a short burst of bluster, James would have done just that. But the weather forecast for the rest of the week reported more of the same: a miserable stream of gales and storms battering the North Sea. If we didn't set sail, we could be sitting on our backsides in Lerwick a week later, and that wasn't ideal for either James or his crew. We'd been fishing for six days and were desperate to get home to Peterhead. The last thing any of us wanted to do was stay put in Lerwick for any great length of time.

James decided we'd set sail.

On the surface it might seem not to be such a wise decision.

But we could see where the skipper was coming from. By sailing out we could get some more fishing done, hopefully reeling in a sizeable haul, return two or three days later to port and unload our fish to a buoyant market. I was beginning to understand, from observing the skipper, the unusual mentality of a captain. He can't afford to think like a mate or a member of the crew in the bilges. He's got to look at the wider picture and weigh up the business as a whole, putting his feelings, whether he's tired or scared, to one side. If he gets the calls right, the crew love him. And if he gets them wrong, well . . .

Off we sailed, steaming out as the storm was fully on us, blowing what we skippers in Peterhead call a hoolie, a powerful surge of gale-force wind. I went on watch. Although I'd been able to go on watch a few times, my experience was limited, to say the least. The *Fidelia* left the comfort of Lerwick port and began pitching and rolling with the swell of the sea. We ran into what's known in the trade as a quartering sea, where the waves pile down on the ship's quarter – the side of the boat toward the stern and halfway down along the keel line, forcing her to rise and tilting the boat to her port side. There's always a risk in such conditions that if you get a big wave, the seas will push into the quarter side of the boat and she'll actually begin to slide down the wave and finish up going broadside, like a surfer stacking it on a surfboard. When a boat's lying on her broadside it's called a broach.

I'd read and heard about what the sea was capable of. But I'd never witnessed it with my own eyes.

We headed into a sea of shuddering darkness, like going into a hollow, empty barn. I sat in the wheelhouse feeling pretty scared. I couldn't see the water. Barely saw anything in front of me in the wheelhouse, save a few small instrument lights glowing like embers. The coal black of the sky melted into the sea and the join was invisible. But I heard its raging. The wind howled as it hit the rigging, screaming at it and shaking it. Spray was flung across the glass in sharp hisses. I thought, something's not right out there. I'd never seen the North Sea in such a bleak and brooding mood.

I was scared, for sure. Scared to the point where I was afraid to slow the boat, as the mannie had told me to stick to a certain speed. You're taught to do whatever the skipper tells you, but a crewman needs a fair amount of common sense and know-how to do his job properly. Regardless of James's instructions, I should've known to slow the boat in, because that's the standard practice when a boat is faced with such a catastrophic storm.

We steamed ahead.

The sea came.

It rose up from the blackness. Tremendous waves, tons and tons of ferocious sea, towering over the wheelhouse, over the *Fidelia*, and suddenly I felt very, very small. And very, very vulnerable.

The waves crashed down, right on top of the wheelhouse.

I heard an ear-snapping bang, and the wheelhouse windows coloured brilliant white. A moment ago they'd been dark as the belly of a cave, and now they were so white you could fool a man into thinking it'd snowed out on deck. The wave rocked the boat violently, and our two hundred tons of steel seemed insignificant against the power of the sea. The *Fidelia* pitched more intensely now, rolling like a cork in a pot of boiling water; we were still steaming ahead at full speed, I was terrified, my hands shaking, and I'd no idea where this lump of water had come from. I hadn't seen any warning of it. It was as if it just sprang out of the sea like a fist, pummelling our little boat.

The boat broached.

I could hear everything rattling within the galley, like each object was becoming possessed. Cups, plates, cutlery – whatever wasn't lashed down was on the move, and moving fast. The energy of the water relentlessly cascaded down on top of the boat, ton after ton of natural force, overpowering us. Plates smashed, knives and forks clattered into one another; the rattling din worsened as the *Fidelia* moved closer and closer to her beam ends, the angle steep, forty-five degrees, and the thought flashed across my mind: *I'm going to die.*

The decks flushed. Water coursed through the galley door, turning the deck into a violent river. The roar of water was all around me, blasting my ears.

The impact of a lump of water lasts seconds. Perhaps one or two. Sometimes it's not even that; it can be just milliseconds. It may not seem like a lot, but when you're on the receiving end of a wave, those small moments seem to stretch on for ever. At the same time, you have this terrible realisation in your guts that you're not in control of the boat; the wave is. It's true what they say, by the way: your life really does pass before your eyes. You're already thinking ahead to your death, and how long it'll take, whether you might drown or freeze, and if so, will it be peaceful? Or perhaps you'll suffer. Will anyone ever find me? I don't want to die.

All these thoughts – they come quick, fast as the lump of water, colliding in your brain at the same time, and you cannot focus on one of them. You're just aware of these things as everything around you threatens to break apart.

While the boat was broached, I'd still kept her going at full speed.

The *Fidelia* swayed. I could feel the dramatic energy of the waves, like an electrical current. The boat unable to maintain its course and keeling over, but drawing on every ounce of its two hundred tons of steel to cope with the pressure the sea applied against it. And then, in the passing of another second, she slowly returned upright, like a dazed boxer picking himself up off the canvas. As she levelled out, torrents of water surged all around the wheelhouse. Water poured down the vents.

I was in a state of pure shock, awestruck by the storm beating around me. I was pinned to that seat, unable to move, like a deer caught in the headlights of an onrushing car.

As the boat struggled to right itself, James Donn had woken up. He'd obviously felt the boat swaying and knew that something bad was afoot, especially seeing as water had piled into the cabin. He came up the stairs to get to the wheelhouse and the sea flooded down on top of him, drenching him through and through. Finally he managed to climb up, where he found me speechless and frozen to the spot. First thing that he did was pull the handle back and turn the wheel to get her up through the wind and start dodging the waves. That told me the skipper was more than a little shook up himself. But somehow I think he wasn't as rigid with fear as I was that night.

We now had a boat that James had to fight to get back on course; the sea had swamped it. We held on at a slow pace. Finally, I was able to breathe a sigh of relief. Everybody else had crawled out of bed and staggered towards the galley, fixing a smoke and a cup of tea to get rid of the shakes.

I went to sleep in my bunk that night – or, I should say, I tried to sleep but couldn't help revisiting the storm. I wasn't sure I could survive another experience like that.

Maybe if I'd been a more experienced sailor, I wouldn't have been so terrified that night on the wheelhouse. I truly thought I was about to meet my Maker. Every fisherman has a moment when he's confronted by the awful power of a storm or a lump of water. From that day onwards, I had the greatest respect for the sea. I never forgot how close we came to being another number. A set of also-rans, lost for ever.

That respect – call it wariness – stays with me to this day. I'm not afraid to go *to* sea, but I'm scared *at* sea. I know the sea has a greater force and energy than any boat or man can throw at it. Somehow you have to push that fear to one side, otherwise you'll not focus on the task of fishing. The fear is sort of like a toothache. When you're there in the middle of it, you make a promise to yourself to give up the fishing if you happen to return to port in one piece. Then you get back, and it doesn't seem so bad. You put it to the back of your mind, and carry on with your job.

A few times in recent years, when I've been sailing through the breakwaters, I've had thoughts along the lines of, Will I be the one who doesn't return home this time? It's not an overwhelming terror, more a fleeting glimpse of what that fear might look like. And maybe a gentle reminder to myself that, for all the hi-tech equipment on board and improved safety, the risks of going out are still very, very high. It's just you, Mother Nature, and one wave.

One wave.

I've sometimes imagined how the boats go, when they do get lost, and I've come to the conclusion that it's not a sequence of waves that forces a boat down, but one wave that has just the right amount of power and height and roll, the kind of wave that doesn't deal in second chances. My good friend and fellow skipper Sandy Watt, who I've known for several years, sometimes nudges my memory. We'll be reminiscing about the old times and he'll say:

'Ken, remind when ye first got a fright at sea?'

'Oh aye,' I'll reply. 'Like it was yesterday.'

What with the storms and the seasickness and the skills, it took me more than a year to earn my sea legs, to the point where if I was clutching a basket of fish, I instinctively reacted with the roll of the boat. As for the seasickness, I struggled on with that until one day I realised, It's all in the mind. When you're busy on deck, the sickness disappears. But when you've got an idle mind and time to sit around below deck, that's when it can strike you. I made it my goal to be occupied as much as possible.

I wanted to be busy for reasons other than coping with seasickness. My desire was to be one of the lads. With the first haul of the morning, when there'd be no fish on deck, I still had to go out and look after the ropes. Even though these same ropes were being winched down into the rope bins, someone had to be in attendance while the rest of the crew were sitting comfortable in the galley, smoking cigarettes and yarning, all joviality and fun. I never looked on tasks like these in a negative way, though. I was driven to become one of the crew and be in the same position as them, on a full share and enjoying the fruits of life at sea. Then some other young lad could be doing the chores I was used to.

I'd joined the *Fidelia* at the same level as I'd been on the *Responsive*, on a half-share, only making half the pay of every other guy in the crew. It took me the best part of two years to progress to a full share. I liked to think of it as an apprenticeship, and if I went about my work eagerly, the skipper might take note of me.

From early morning to late at night, I put everything into getting ahead on that boat. When I was forward and at the first haul of the day, I'd get an old length of rope and start to learn to splice.

Bearing in mind that this splice had to go down through a coiler, the pressure was on to make sure I produced a nice, neat splice. My splices in the early days were utterly terrible, things that looked like an elephant's trunk, and when the mate came forward and saw my handiwork, he'd grab the splice from me and hit me around the legs with it, shouting, 'Not good enough! Do it again!'

I'd be angry and hurt, tears welling in my eyes, but deep down I'd know the mate was right. I had to improve dramatically before my splicing would be up to scratch. And when you're out there at sea, you're in a man's world. There's no mother to go crying to, no one to rely on for help but yourself. Pride kicks in too, because no one wants to be known as the guy who cannot splice. The mate finished giving me an earful and took off. I'd fetch another bit of old rope and start all over again. Keep practising until I got it right. Unlike the other chores I was given, splicing wasn't about pure physical strength, but the skills with your hands. Old rope was set aside for me to try and splice.

Like everything else, there's a secret to splicing, and practice definitely makes perfect.

On seine-net vessels, a coil of rope is 220 metres long. A series of spliced coils – twenty-six in all, spliced together – were shot off the deck as the vessel steamed ahead at full speed, setting the gear. It only took one dodgy bit of spliced rope to spoil the haul, as the ropes would foul up the coiler mechanism when being winched back up. So a great deal of splicing and maintenance needed to be carried out on the ropes. The crew kept a continual eye on each splice, looking for weak spots and putting them aside so they could be replaced. The oldest saying in our industry is, *A skipper's only as good as his gear.* Top skippers had top crews working underneath them, every guy keeping a firm eye on this vital bit of rope.

I had to hack into the rope using a sharpened knife, opening out both ends of the rope I needed to splice, and the next step was to merge the ends into one another and splice it back together as a single, very durable rope. Imagine untwisting two lengths of rope and then interweaving their strands. It sounds easy, but if you started out wrong, the splice would stay wrong. It didn't sort itself out. If the splice was too big, it'd stick in the coiler mechanism as the rope was winched back on board, a mistake that was liable to incur a tongue-lashing from the skipper.

Getting up to scratch was immensely satisfying, and once I could splice properly, I'd challenge my colleagues for a bit of fun. Maybe there'd be a couple of splices to go into the ropes; me and the next youngest lad would compete to see who'd finish first, the mate and the rest of the crew goading us on, shouting out, 'Ah, yer rubbish, I'll bet ye cannae put that splice together in five minutes.'

I've mentioned about taking a watch in the wheelhouse on the *Responsive*. On the *Fidelia* I received an education on the finer points of the maritime highway code, more complex than the basic red–light–to–red–light principle. Navigating by compass, basic chart work such as finding your position on a map, watching engine temperatures and alarms . . . the list of things going on while you're on watch is staggering.

By far the biggest challenge was merely keeping my eyes open. I had the mate on my case all the time, trying to catch me out by disappearing into the engine room and sneaking back up to see if I was still alert. And pity the poor soul caught cat-napping; an ear-bashing and a boot up the backside would follow, sure as night follows day. I'd be ridiculed in front of the crew at breakfast the next morning too. Watch-keeping lasted anything from one to five hours, and coming on the back of a long day, all you really wanted was to curl up in bed and get some rest.

On some days the fishing might only stop for three hours. Once we'd sorted the catch I was left with two hours' sleep, split into an hour apiece for me and my colleague. Those hours were the worst. I was so utterly knackered that I'd dive into my bunk for fifteen minutes and wake up with drool running down the side of my open mouth. I used to go up on deck, smoke a cigarette to clear my head and prepare myself for another eighteen-hour shift. I think every other challenge life at sea has thrown at me, seasickness or splicing, has gotten easier over the years. With sleep, it's the opposite. When you're a young lad, you can get by on two hours' kip, it's nae a problem.

'Wait till yer fifty,' one of the old salts told me one day. 'Ye'll ken all about it then.'

Now I'm there, I know the guy was right. There are chronic aches in my joints; my legs and arms creak and strain like rusted old doors. My body bears the scars of thirty-five years as a hunter at sea. Thirty-five years of riding storms and slogging a full day's work – a *real* full day – have taken their toll.

Living as a half-share, I spent most of my time with a lump in my throat, a tightness in my belly and a tear in my eye. I think my ears must've looked like cauliflowers in that first year, the number of mistakes I made along the way. Two things kept me going. One, I was keen as mustard. And two, I knew that every other man on that boat, from the skipper and the mate down to the crew, had once been a young lad. They'd climbed out of the hole and if I stayed focused on the work and paid attention to everything going on around me, I'd be out soon enough.

Grabbing that full share – I tell you, that was the best feeling in the world.

6

MAIDEN VOYAGE

With life improving at sea, things took a turn for the better ashore too, when I met my future wife.

Irene was an incredibly attractive twenty-year-old. When we first met I was struck by the stunning blue eyes that radiated from her face; eyes that both my daughters have inherited. Somehow I managed to convince her to go on a date with me. At the end I thought, Okay Jimmy, best play this cool, you don't want to look too keen. When the time came to go our separate ways I smiled and said plainly, 'Well . . . see you around.'

My tactic must have worked – or so I thought – because she agreed to go out on a second date. Sure enough, at the end of the night, Irene turned to me, gave me a casual smile and said, 'Well . . . see you around.'

The scores even, our friendship and love for one another quickly blossomed. I think we're a very lucky couple, as we have a tremendous amount in common and have always got on well together. Irene has very strong convictions and speaks her mind, a habit which has saved me more than once in my career. Although she didn't come from a fishing background, her father worked away from home, so she was familiar with living in a household where the burden was largely on the mother to bring up the family, and that probably made it a wee bit easier for her when I was out at sea. Irene was the one who encouraged me to grasp every opportunity that came my way, and to never waver from my dreams, and I truly think we were made for each other.

I loved the fact that Irene spoke her mind, and wasn't afraid to make instant decisions. I like to think we work well as a team – I run the business and she's in charge of the household, and while we don't see eye-to-eye on every little detail, we do know how to get on well together. We just clicked. And a skipper couldn't wish for a more loving, caring and understanding woman at the family helm. Irene never interfered with my sailing schedule or moaned about the time I spent at sea. She understood that I had to make some tough commercial decisions in the best interests of the business and my crew. She had to cope with the lonely weeks bringing up the children while I was out at sea, but she never once complained.

We decided to get engaged in September 1982.

By 1983, I'd saved enough money to buy an old house in the village of Buchanhaven – the same place my kin came from, and which later became part of the town of Peterhead. I suppose you'd call it a typical first-time property: the house cost me a little over £3,000 and was in need of a few repairs and a fresh lick of paint. My father said he'd lend a hand and I applied to the local council for a grant so that we could build a kitchen and an indoor toilet – the place was that old that its toilet was an outdoor feature, not something my bride-to-be was ready to embrace with open arms.

I received some bad news when I discovered that the granite-built house had foundation problems and I wouldn't be able to apply for a grant for a property with structural defects. Before I could get the grant, I needed to come up with more than £7,000 for the essential repairs. I was shocked – and bewildered. Granite buildings were supposed to last for ever, and Peterhead was world-famous for its rock deposits; they'd helped construct the London Stock Exchange and Southwark Bridge across the Thames.

More bad news followed: I was informed that the building was located in the middle of a special conservation area. Eventually I became frustrated with the whole situation and contacted my Member of Parliament, a man by the name of Albert Macquarrie, and wrote him a letter outlining my predicament. I'm not sure what I was expecting – but within a couple of weeks, my local council came back to me saying that a grant would be made available for the repairs to the structural damage of the house. Mr Macquarrie himself took the trouble to write to me too – a wonderful gesture.

Fully repaired, this was the home Irene and I were married into, in April 1984. Now I had settled down into family life, the risks I was running every time I went out to sea were focused clearly in my mind. I didn't have to think only about my welfare, but that of my wife, and, soon enough, my daughters.

The trouble with doing a dangerous job is that after a while, you run the risk of dropping your guard. Hazards become the norm; risks to your life, part of the everyday routine.

As the *Fidelia*'s ropes were winched back on to the deck, they'd run only a few feet from the area where we gutted and washed the catch. Sometimes the ropes would be running over my head as I transferred the fish into the fishroom. The ropes were so taut that I'd hear them pinging and cracking with the tension as they ran overhead, having to resist more than 2,000 pounds per square inch of pressure when retrieving the gear. It was a mammoth task and the ropes seemed to demonstrate their anger: they deposited small particles of sand they'd carried up from the seabed on to the nape of your neck and your hair, which caused every deck hand a great deal of chafing and discomfort. Worse, if the ropes were to break under the intense tensile stress, the backlash would not only take me out in one clean blow, but any other unlucky soul who happened to be nearby. Ropes might not look dangerous, but every fisherman's aware of how lethal they can be.

The catch was retrieved on to the deck in deck ponds. From there it was our job to scoop up tons of fish – by hand – into empty fish boxes in preparation for gutting. A good haul meant the job of scooping fish tired the crew out even before the long task of gutting the catch had begun. And once the catch was on board, the skipper would start shooting his ropes for the next haul. I really had to watch my step – tense ropes running above me, and a deck flush with slippery fish, some of them near sliding overboard with the roll of the boat.

In the cold of winter one year we set sail for a trip. With daylight hours extremely limited, we made a bearing north towards the Shetland Isles. We knew darkness would set in early in the day and, with no time to waste, it was full speed, giving it everything we had. The day was fresh and a near-gale force wind had whipped up, when James Donn hit a good patch of fish. Brilliant. The crew were delighted. But word soon spread about the patch and suddenly James was locked in a battle to out-shoot his comrades, who by now were all jostling to get their ropes and nets in the water. James was frantically shooting the gear as fast as he could. His focus on the task at hand was total.

While James busied himself with landing more bountiful catches, we were on deck and getting down to the business of scooping and stowing the catch as best we could. Our job wasn't made any easier by the fact that the *Fidelia* kept dipping her rail, causing us to lose a few baskets of fish. As a seine-net fishery, the gear was set on the seabed in a triangular pattern, meaning we had to make a series of major alterations in course. Each time we rounded, the *Fidelia* took another deep lurch into the swell, and more of the fish on deck disappeared over the rails. We increased the pace, scooping like mad in order to box as much fish as possible before we rounded what's known as a 'bight' – a body of water shaped like an indent on the coast line. We needed to complete a series of bights to set the ropes.

With the nets shot and just one final bight to clear, we'd done a fine job in clearing almost all the fish off the deck, more than fifty boxes in total all stowed up, wedged in and ready for the last leg back to the dhan buoy attached to one end of the ropes. The dhan is at the beginning of the ropes. We started to set on the seabed. As we rounded the last corner we made back to the dhan buoy in order to complete the triangular shape to make a seine-net haul. Everything looked good.

Out of nowhere, a freak wave broke over the vessel's shoulder. Now, normally the guys will see a wave coming. You notice it in the distance, rolling up like a liquid avalanche, building momentum. This one literally burst from the sea, stunning the crew.

In these days the *Fidelia* had an open-ended shelter deck. This was the first type of protection afforded crewmen on what was mainly an open-deck ship. A shelter deck wasn't fully enclosed – the front and back of it was always open, sort of like a pigsty without the ends to it.

Even within this shelter deck, we had no protection against

the wave. It wouldn't go over us – the freakish thing was going to go *through* us. Batter the guys on deck.

Daylight shut down. Darkness rushed us as the ferocious, solid lump of water came crashing towards the forward end of the deck. We looked at each other. Knew that the wave would break around us and leave by the rear exit, taking anything lying in its destructive path. We felt the power of the water, a tremendous energy trapped within it. Energy that could swipe a grown man off his feet and cast him aside, like a balloon being set free in the sky.

No time to shout or take evasive action. The wave acted like a twister about to shred your home. You cannot outrun such a thing. It is coming at you, whether you like it or not.

The wave struck.

I grabbed on to the handrail, clinging for dear life. The wave worked its wrath. Boxes of fish, men; everything on deck was floating. I didn't have time to look out for my crew-mates; the situation was dire, we could be washed overboard and it was every man for himself.

As the wave engulfed us the intensity of its cold took my breath away. It felt like a double-whammy: ice-cold water freezing my bones, and the terrifying shock of seeing a sudden sea hurtling across the deck, blinding me. For a fleeting second I didn't know if I was on board or washed overboard. I had no lifejacket, just my oilskins and boots filled to the brim with salt water. I remember, most clearly, a feeling of total fear.

If I get swept off, I'm probably not coming back.

The wave swept through us, devastating the deck. I looked up and saw two of my crew-mates in the fish ponds, now emptied of fish. They were swimming for dear life inside these miniature pools, disorientated by the chaotic tide of water flooding them.

Finally the wave passed, and I gathered my senses. Half the catch had been washed overboard, along with the boxes it was stowed in. A quick head-count established that all the crew had survived, dulled heads and legs popping up all over the deck. We were soaked through and wide-eyed with shock. No one had expected such a dramatic lump. One of the crew reckoned we'd been hit by a lump just as its surf was poised to break over itself. Whatever the cause of the wave, every man understood the message loud and clear: life-threatening situations don't only happen in stormy weather. Sure, the water hadn't been flat calm, but we'd seen plenty of rougher days at sea. We hadn't thought there was any risk of being washed overboard by a huge lump of sea.

Another reminder from the sea of how dangerous our job really was.

In 1979, having progressed to a full share on *Fidelia*, I began taking an active interest in the engineering side of the boat. I'd been fascinated by machinery since I was a young boy, and it wasn't long before I was channelling my curiosity into the mysterious workings of the engine room. My eldest brother, David, studied mathematics and physics at university; my other older brother, Pete, was an electrician and electronics wizard like my father. Maybe some kind of interest in systems and how they work rubbed off on me. I absolutely loved helping out the ship's engineer. Each ship had a dedicated engineer. Although he mucked in with deck work, his most important job was to look after the machinery.

James the skipper was, I suspect, halfway thrown by my sudden obsession with engineering. But it made me stand out from the crowd as someone who was serious about studying every aspect of a boat, and he encouraged me to work and learn with the engineer.

I started off by doing what I'd normally do on the *Fidelia* – offer a hand whenever he needed it. I'd help him with the greasing and changing the oil and such. In those days a lot of things were belt-driven, and we were forever having to tighten up loosened belts and recognise the tell-tale signs that a belt was suffering from excessive wear and tear. I didn't do these jobs in order to garner favour with the skipper, though. I did it because I enjoyed it.

I spent an increasing amount of time downstairs, below deck, learning about winches and engines and – the most important task – how to sort out choked pumps, as these were the things that kept us afloat. A boat is fitted with pumps to keep the bilges dry. The bilges are the rounded element of the ship's hull and are located as a separate compartment on the end side of the keel, the main structure of the hull. Put simply, the bilges consume excess water.

It was common to get a build-up of water inside the bilges, due to spillage from the fishroom and rough seas. Basically, any water that doesn't drain off the side of the deck goes down into the bilges, and these need to be pumped daily at sea. There were two pumps to each compartment and they'd choke from time to time, or there'd be a problem getting a pump to function properly.

The work was a welcome break from the endless routine of shooting nets, hauling and gutting. I learned valuable insights into the insides of the ship. Knowledge that would stand me in good stead for years to come. Indeed, I was so interested in this work that when James promoted the engineer to first mate, I took on the role of ship's engineer.

Through my taking on that job, James came to see me as a valuable member of the crew. I was a young guy, full of beans, gaining expert knowledge on the workings of the boat and how to fix mechanical failures; and the fact that I lived in Peterhead was a big bonus too, as it meant that they had some-one on hand, five minutes up the road, who could tend to the boat in port, what with the crew all living in Fraserburgh.

Skipper Donn pulled me aside one day ashore.

'Ken, we like ye, we see yer hard working, we git on well with ye . . .' He paused. 'How would ye like to own a share of *Fidelia*?'

I was over the moon.

It was the tradition that, if a guy was loyal and hard-work-ing, then somewhere down the line he'd be offered the part ownership of a vessel. Back then, a ship's crew weren't just men who gutted fish and shot rope. Some were also shareholders – in the ship they worked on.

Being a *shareholder* is different to being a half or full share. The share is a fisherman's wage – the money he works for, because he gets a share of the vessel's catch. Whereas buying into a share of the vessel means a fisherman becomes a part owner of the business. He enters into a partnership with the skipper and the other guys who have been offered shareholder stakes. The advantages for a fisherman in becoming a share-holder are that he gets collateral in the boat. He doesn't get it for free – he has to pay for it, same as buying shares in any com-pany. But he now has a vested interest in the future of the boat and, should the vessel be sold on several years later at a profit, he'll receive a healthy return on the money he put down. It was this collateral that enabled me to finally get to own my first boat.

A boat was divided up into sixty-four shares, and these shares were grouped into sixteenths. Two thirty-twos was a six-teenth. What James Donn was offering me was two sixteenths, which works out as an eighth of a boat – nothing, really, in the grand scheme of things, but it sure felt like a big deal to a wee lad who'd not long ago found his sea legs.

In order to secure my eighth, I had to have the money. I didn't have it to hand, but luckily for me, they arranged for me to borrow the money through the bank. This was the norm back then. I got a bill of sale which stated that I had a two-sixteenths shareholding in the *Fidelia*. I'd come a long way in a short space of time. There was no sitting on my laurels, though. I was hungry for more success. If anything, owning a part of the boat made me even more driven to succeed. I was willing to do as much as possible to try and save the business money.

Whatever chore needed doing, I'd volunteer for it. Any time I'd go down to the quay and do the chore myself if required, rather than go to the fuss of calling a tradesman in. I guess, from James Donn's point of view, it was win–win. He got a lad with the bit between his teeth, and guaranteed his future to the boat with his eighth share.

I knew the mate I'd replaced as engineer on the *Fidelia* well and I was able to watch him very closely. He was the skipper's brother and he'd skipper the boat when James went off on holiday. Eventually he left to buy his own boat, and I thought to myself, Well now. Here's the chance to get my own ticket.

I'd only been married a few months, and now I decided it was high time I gained my mate's certificate. I enrolled at Banff & Buchan College in neighbouring Fraserburgh and joined a class of about twenty guys, all super keen to become fully qualified mates. To graduate from a crew hand to a mate, you had to complete a twelve-week course, or eight weeks if you took up the option to take early exams. (Nowadays these courses last for about six months.) As money was tight and all my assets were tied up in the house in Buchanhaven, I knew I couldn't afford to be slack when it came to my studies or my work.

While at college I busted a gut to soak up the information. Failure was not an option.

The mate's course was hard work and good fun. Every day I learned something new, from two-page-long sums instructing me how to steer by the sun with a sextant, to understanding Morse code at a fast pace. We also had to memorise the 'rules of the road' inside out, reading a thick book which contained every little law and protocol at sea. A fierce rivalry simmered beneath the surface between me and my classmates as we jostled to earn the best grades in the class. I found myself in a surreal situation; back in school, I'd never bothered about being top of the class. All of a sudden, I became obsessed by my grades.

There was a lot of learning to be done. I was thankful for all the times my skippers had demonstrated the rules of the road to me, as it meant that I had some of the book's laws tucked away in my mind before I'd even flipped to the first page. James had been aware of my desire to take the mate's exam for a while, and he took the time to give me some pointers. He realised how tough the college course was, and that the more learning I could cram in prior to the course, the greater my chance of passing.

When it came to Morse code, I held a cheeky advantage over the other guys, because my mother was giving me a bit of home tuition. Prior to meeting my father, she'd worked as a telegraphist with the General Post Office (GPO) in Stornoway on the Isle of Lewis in the Outer Hebrides.

Naturally she read Morse quickly and accurately, so I had to have my wits about me.

She'd set me a task, drawing up Morse code puzzles for me to crack – a block of numerals and letters from the alphabet which required my full concentration, and she'd finish by sending me a message that I had to translate. Here I did cheat a little: after a while, I figured out that the message was the headline of that day's local paper. From then on, I took the trouble to catch the paper's front page before I went along for my Morse code tuition. My mother thought I was really good at the messages.

Now she knows!

Aside from the Morse code, there were so many new things to learn in the classes that I found it impossible to absorb everything we were taught; I had to spend many hours at home, staying up till late in the evening, going over and over the work until it was burned into my memory. Making it doubly hard was the fact that, all the time I was doing the course, I wasn't going to sea and earning a pay. A small bursary barely covered my expenses on cigarettes and petrol, so I'd boost my income by going down to the port and helping out with landing the *Fidelia* when she came in. On the plus side, it was great to be able to spend some precious time with Irene, going to bed in my own home every night.

A few weeks into the course, Irene became sick and had the worst of it in the mornings. We both suspected the reason, but she confirmed it to me one day when I came back from college. She was pregnant.

A big, big smile broke out across my face. Sure, I was off work, not earning money, we had no cash surplus to support us, but the news that a baby was on the way made me beam with happiness. I felt life was coming together; everything was going to be okay. Irene and I would always have each other, and that's more important than having a few extra pennies.

Still, I put pressure on myself to get back to work. I wanted to give my children the life I'd maybe not had as a kid, and excited as I was about Irene's pregnancy, the news also made passing the mate's certificate more urgent. I applied to sit my exams early, after eight weeks rather than the normal twelve, hoping that my long hours of studying were about to pay off. With no small amount of trepidation, I took the exam, and was delighted to be told that I'd passed. I gained two certificates – a mate's qualification, and a special certificate that permitted me to go to sea as skipper, one level above the mate. In addition, I was licensed to skipper a vessel up to a certain size.

Certificates in my back pocket, I set about using my new-found skills to get a chance to skipper the *Fidelia*. The ship's mate had departed to buy his own boat, and this propelled me to make the final push and achieve my goal. For the past few years I'd been lucky to watch James Donn up close, trying to understand his mindset and why he chose one route over another. My confidence was always strong, and now I'd become a mate, I truly believed I was hungry for a taste of the wheelhouse action.

Each morning I'd go up to the wheelhouse and ask questions of James, finding out what he was doing and why. Usually he was a good teacher; he patiently explained to me why we were shooting our gear in a certain place. Other times he was in the zone, totally focused on the task at hand, and it'd be up to me to suss out his strategy. At night I'd pore over the maps, looking at where we'd fished that day and where we were headed for the next day, trying to absorb this mental map of the North Sea. Sometimes I'd look at what he was doing and think to myself, I'd not do it this way, maybe I'd do this or that differently.

To navigate around the complex waters of the North Sea, James referred to massive cardboard charts three feet by four. He had hundreds of the things. I knew that if I wanted to get to know the sea inside out, where all the good shots and bad areas were to be found, the wrecks and obstructions on the seabed that could potentially shred your gear – well, I'd have to copy these maps. By hand.

So it was that, each weekend ashore, I'd cart a couple of maps home, acquire some cardboard of a similar size, and draw a painstakingly detailed replica of James's original. This task ate up most of my weekends, at times when I was knackered after a trip and wanted to do nothing more than relax and spend time with Irene. I took great care to copy them exactly: each map represented part of the skipper's many years of knowledge.

It took me two years to copy all the maps. Nowadays a potential 'mannie' can shove a USB stick into my PC and download all my maps in five minutes, hey presto. That's progress for you.

When you're chasing your dream, I have discovered, you cannot go wrong by gathering intelligence and information from those around and above you. I ached to be a skipper, and I made it my business to observe James, as well as the other skippers at port, whenever the opportunity presented. As 1984 turned into '85, making a success out of my career became even more urgent with the birth of our first daughter Jenna. Now I had a young family to look after, I pursued my dream harder than ever. That same year, I at last got my chance to try my hand as a skipper.

Jenna's birth brought joy to me and Irene, and also had a special significance to our parents. Neither of our families had young children – Jenna was the first grandchild on my side of the family, and although there were grandchildren on Irene's side, they were all grown up. We had no immediate cousins or nephews, and none of our friends had yet started a family. Basically, we had no one to ask about the ins and outs of looking after a baby. Our collective knowledge amounted to nappies and milk.

On the day we took Jenna home from the hospital, the nurse carried her out to the car. Irene climbed into the back, the nurse gently handing Jenna into her arms. I paced around to the front, got into the driver's seat and fired up the engine. As I made to reverse, I glanced at the rear-view mirror and clocked Irene's striking blue eyes staring back at me as she cradled Jenna. She had a certain look on her face. Not a word passed between us, but I knew what was on her mind, because I was thinking exactly the same thing.

What do we do now, then?

We had to make it up as we went along. I like to think Irene and I made a reasonable job of it.

My badgering of James paid off one fine day in July 1985. I was at home when James phoned me up out of the blue and said he was going on a trip away and would I like to take the *Fidelia* out? For the last couple of months James had been tutoring me in shooting and hauling the gear, and I kind of sensed that the time was almost right for me to do the skipper's role. Now my dream had come true. This was the real deal. Jimmy Buchan, skipper. Had a certain ring to it.

A funny thing happened as I steered the boat between the pier heads: all the brash confidence and grand ideas I had for the boat suddenly evaporated. The thought dawned on me that I was in charge of this vessel. I had the responsibility of navigating the boat to the right area and catching a haul of fish, and my reputation was on the line. Fail in my task and I could surely forget about being a skipper ever again. The pressure was like nothing else I'd ever experienced.

The North Sea, I have discovered, can be an unforgiving place to work. It doesn't care whether you're in dire need of a good catch or are down on your luck; it can crush a man, has the power to make or break a skipper. As we headed deep into the sea that first day, my yield was terrible: a few boxes, nowhere near enough to cover our daily overheads. The pressure mounted. You've got to deliver, Jimmy, I told myself. Think positive and it'll come good.

On the second day I picked a new area to farm.

We suffered another terrible catch.

There's no worse feeling for a skipper than returning thin catch after thin catch. He becomes aware of the crew losing faith, and once the crew no longer believes in the captain's ability, he's a dead man walking. The faces of my crew said it all. They were glum and etched with worry. These were guys I'd spent ten years alongside as a deck hand, and yet now I felt totally isolated from them up in the wheelhouse.

'On the deck you work from the shoulders down; in the wheelhouse, you work from the shoulders up,' one of the crew told me.

Charming, I thought. *I really am on my own.*

As a mate, I had all the answers. If the skipper made a blunder, I'd soon know about it. The way I saw it, I'd done my apprenticeship. I'd changed the oils and studied the maps and I'd been awarded my certificate. I knew everything there was to know.

At least, I thought I did.

On the third evening I instinctively looked behind me, to the spot James would stand when he was showing me the ropes . . . and realised I was all alone in the wheelhouse, and maybe not the know-it-all I'd assumed. In fact, I was as green as a pea. The crew weren't interested in my problems upstairs. They just hankered to do the job and go home.

'Ooph,' I said to myself. 'I'm really stuck.'

By day four we'd accumulated a measly fifty boxes. I tried to keep my spirits high and steamed further offshore, reasoning that fortune favours the brave and it was preferable to be proactive than cursing my bad luck.

In those days, with no hi-tech navigation system, I simply drew a line on the chart indicating where I wanted us to go, informed the watch keeper and went to catch some vital kip. At three o'clock in the morning, a distraught crew member shouted down to me that he had no idea where we were, as the navigator had gone crazy. I raced up to the wheelhouse to look for myself and he was bang on the money: the navigator, which relied on radio waves to mark position fixes, was flashing wildly. The three positions on the clocks were twirling like the rotors on a helicopter. I had no idea why; it was on the blink. We were as good as lost: I had no idea where we were.

Daybreak was almost upon us and I couldn't be sure about our location; we weren't in the area we were supposed to be in. Back when I'd been a deck hand, navigation had never been a concern for me. I merely took it for granted that the skipper knew what he was doing. The boot was on the other foot now. I had a big responsibility to pull us out of this mess and get on with the business of fishing.

I thought that at least we could catch the first haul, which would last for two hours. That would take us through to daybreak. In full daylight I'd be able to get a fix on where I thought I was by steaming at full speed north. If the waters deepened then I'd know that my water depth and position matched, providing me with a fix on the charts. We arrived at the edge of this water, a good mark came over the echo sounder that was used to locate fish, and I breathed a huge sigh of relief. Not only were we on course – I had a chance to make a catch too. The *Fidelia* was on the edge of the deep body of water, the one I'd identified as an area that might be home to a large haul of fish. I shot the nets, timing it perfectly as I marked the shoal of fish all the way.

I had no idea what kind of fish I'd caught. On the one hand it might be lucrative whitefish like cod and haddock; if Lady Luck wasn't shining on me, it might be feeding fish like sand eels and such. Only time would tell.

Lassoing the area with my seine-net ropes, I steered back to the marker buoy and started heaving in the gear. I was impatient to see the results of the catch, but I stuck to my training and hauled the nets in slowly – heave too quickly and your gear won't fish correctly. Vessel speed and gear tension were critical. I crossed my fingers. This was it. Make or break. Either I turned in a good catch at last, or the crew would forever doubt my ability to be a skipper. My reputation would be in tatters.

Adrenalin pumping, I chained cigarettes one after the other, running out on to the deck to check that the gear was drawing in correctly, darting back into the wheelhouse to speed up the winch – just a wee bit, mind, no point in overdoing it – and generally in a state of massive anxiety. I tried not to show it to the crew, but inside the tension had my stomach bound up in tense knots.

After almost an hour the ropes had closed together. Finally, it was time to heave up the gear. Another cigarette; my mouth tasted like an ashtray. The crew emerged on the deck with their oilskins on, ready to bring in the net. It seemed to take for ever. The net reached the stern of the vessel, while I arrowed from window to window. The echo sounder promised a good haul, but the disasters of the previous days' fishing were clear in my mind and I didn't want to get my hopes up.

As I continued to come astern to ease the burden of hauling the net by the crew, my nerves shredded as I slackened the gear. She rose like a whale out of the water – *whoosh!* – breaking the surface, my eyes searching the cod-end of the nets, the part of the trawl where the fish are retained. The eyes of my crew were glued to the cod-end as well. And as it lifted we saw the catch and I couldn't hold it in any longer, I screamed at the top of my voice, the crew shouting and smiling alongside me.

'We knew you could do it!' they yelled. The previous seventy-two hours were soon forgotten.

Remembering the patience of the skippers I'd worked under, I tried to remain calm as we brought the haul alongside and lifted it on board. A final tug on the cod-line rope – reeved through the cod-end of the nets – and the fish hit the deck, plentiful, good-sized haddock thrashing about, I figured at least eighty boxes' worth of prize whitefish. The rest of the catch was lowered on board and I stood on the deck, not wearing oilskins, up to my waist in beautiful, fresh fish.

No time to waste. With the catch on board, I wanted to shoot away again. That's what being a skipper is all about. A good skipper always wants to shoot his nets, because he knows time without his nets in the sea is wasted time. You're out there to fish, not admire the view.

We settled into a happy pattern for the rest of the trip. My pride had been restored and I felt the hunter instinct more powerfully than ever before. This is what I was born to do. I'd gone toe-to-toe with Mother Nature and come out on top.

Our return to port saw us land a total haul that grossed £10,000 at the fish market: the dream start to my career. In fact, our sales agent went to the trouble of seeking me out to congratulate me on my first trip, which was a nice boost to my self-esteem. I hadn't doubted my ability to get going, and now I reaped the reward.

This trip gave me a hunger for captaining my own vessel. In the back of my mind was the *Fidelia*'s ex-mate and his decision to leave. I got to thinking that perhaps I'd have to follow the same path as him, and sooner rather than later.

I was aware that James Donn had two sons coming, four or five years younger than me. When it came to choosing someone to captain the *Fidelia*, they'd be first in line. I didn't feel angry or upset about this state of affairs; that's just the way life went. If you were a skipper and had a son, you'd pass the boat on to the boy soon as you'd let him inherit your house. But it did bring to mind that the opportunity I had on the *Fidelia* was a small one, and it wasn't going to last for ever.

If I stay here, I told myself, eventually I'll go back to the bilges. And no one ever wants to go back to the bilges once they've got the skippering bug.

My departure from the *Fidelia* came about when James decided he was going to carry out a big conversion to the vessel, one that would come at huge expense. By this time I'd dropped a few hints that I was of a mind to move on to pastures new, and the skipper wanted a commitment from me to help towards the cost of the rebuilding work. The whole conversion would cost hundreds of thousands of pounds, and I would've been taking on two-sixteenths of that debt, under the terms of my share.

'Fitya want to do, to commit, or go?' James asked me.

'I'd rather take my money,' I replied.

Our split was an amicable one. They fixed me a price on the sale of the share that suited us both. After ten years on board *Fidelia* I was leaving to start up on my own with a few thousand to put down on my new venture. This was a big step. My own adventure was about to begin.

7

GREENHORN SKIPPER

We moved house not long after Jenna was born. Although I quite liked living in the area, Irene wasn't exactly over the moon about being stuck out in Buchanhaven and she felt especially isolated when I was at sea.

Things came to a head one day when Irene went to visit her parents with Jenna in the late afternoon and returned home several hours later, as night-time set in. She knew I was due back home that same day and as she drove back to the house, she spied a light on in the front room and assumed I'd returned from the trip a wee bit early. Excited at the prospect of seeing me, Irene ran into the house. She heard a noise coming from upstairs, figured it was me. As she walked down the hallway, however, she realised that the house had been turned upside down: drawers emptied, cupboards overturned. Now she heard the commotion upstairs: the burglar escaping through the upstairs window.

Cold with fright, Irene called the police but the burglar was long gone by the time they arrived.

Needless to say, that night, when I did finally make it through the front door, a stressed Irene told me in no uncertain terms that we'd be moving to a new home much quicker than we'd originally envisaged. The fact she had just had a baby made her experience very distressing, though I must say in hindsight, as a young man I failed to appreciate the fear and the loneliness of living alone. I had grown up with my brothers, then I went to pursue a career in the fishing, which meant sleeping with five or six men to a boat. Really, I'd never slept alone in the house and didn't see things from Irene's point of view until a few years later, when Amy was born. With Irene in hospital, I had to go home with Jenna. I was a twenty-eight-year-old man going back to an empty house for the first time. The strange feeling I experienced that night made me realise how Irene must have felt on occasion raising the girls.

The house was on the market the same weekend as the burglary and sold within a month. Thankfully I made a good return on the property: the work me and my father had invested in renovating and building extensions had increased its value, and the sale of that house allowed us to move to a nice new place on the outskirts of town.

Now I had assets, however, I could borrow money to buy a fishing vessel. I was about to realise my dream.

I purchased the *Amity* in the late summer of 1986 for a very good price from a retiring skipper called David Flett. She was a seventy-foot vessel and at the time easily the best in the fleet. Even today I can still picture the envious looks the other skippers were giving me when I finally took ownership of her. *Amity* was the perfect boat to start my career. I was determined not to fail, and that strength of mind would help me get through some very dark days ahead. But on the day I purchased the *Amity*, worries about my future and the health of the fishing industry couldn't have been further from my mind.

Back in the mid-1980s, Peterhead port was still enjoying the boom years of the fishing industry and the parallel rocket in shipbuilding. Boat yards up and down the region were building fishing vessels flat out. There were yards in Arbroath, Peterhead, Fraserburgh, Macduff and Sandhaven, and two yards in Buckie. Yards in Aberdeen and Campbeltown churned out steel seiners, while the other yards specialised in constructing traditional wooden vessels. Some skippers were even going abroad to build vessels. Except for Macduff, these boat yards are now all closed.

Getting a boat was fairly easy, as there were so many fishing vessels for sale all around the UK; money was always changing hands as each wave of new skippers came along to try their luck in the treacherous North Sea and west coast waters. Some would fall by the wayside, but I promised myself I would not be one of them.

I very nearly didn't buy *Amity* – or *Seaforth*, as she was previously known. I'd been looking at several different vessels for a while and seriously considering one or two others. I was mindful of taking on too much debt from the local bank, so the boats I was looking at were in the £70,000 to £100,000 bracket. For that kind of money I could get myself an older boat that had been subjected to a bit more wear and tear and was maybe slower than some of the newer models. However, my bank manager wasn't so keen on the idea.

'These older boats will let ye down,' he said. I remember thinking that his office was nice and warm, not at all like being out on the boat, where cold winds stung like cold steel pressed against your skin, and your fingers and toes were numb for days on end. 'Why don't ye get a much newer vessel, one that will give ye a lot more years of service, ye ken?'

He was suggesting I spend twice the money on a much newer boat, one that would give me a much better return on my investment. It would mean committing to a bigger debt, but the potential rewards outweighed the risks. It was sound business sense, and a bit of advice I have always been grateful for. At the time, I was stunned, but eager to embrace his proposal.

'Okay, then,' I replied. You don't disagree with the bank manager!

All the skippers in the fleet knew about the *Seaforth*. When I heard a whisper that David Flett was to retire, I knew this was my big chance.

Flush with a bigger loan guarantee from my bank manager, I telephoned Mr Flett and explained who I was: a young lad looking for a start in life, hard-working and honest. I'd heard on the grapevine that he was considering retirement and would he consider selling his boat to me? It's highly unusual for a skipper to sell to a guy ringing him out of the blue like I did. The normal thing to do was to put an advert in the *Fishing News*, a weekly publication for the industry, and give a closing date, selling to the highest bidder.

'We-ell,' he said, 'I *was* thinking of selling my boat . . .'

My luck seemed to be in.

He went on, 'I'm looking for somewhere in the region of a hundred and eighty to two hundred thousand for it.'

I offered the odd sum of £205,000 – the bank manager had given me a salient piece of advice after upping my loan.

'Whatever the boat's worth,' he said, 'offer five thousand more.'

So that's what I did.

After what felt like an hour's pause, he said, 'I'd like to see ye first. How about ye come to my house for tea?'

I confided in one or two people in the industry and asked them if they knew anything about David Flett. They told me that he was right old school, considered to be the admiral of the fleet, and the lads who had served on his crew said he ran a very regimented, disciplined operation. A highly respected man, he was very fair but quite strict, and they told me that if he didn't like me, or got the impression that I would mistreat his beloved boat, then no matter how much money I offered him, he wouldn't sell. Even if I was laying down double the asking price, one wrong word and the chance to own my dream boat would be lost for ever. The most important thing for him was seeing the boat go to a good home.

'I'm telling ye,' a guy said to me. 'Ye can turn up at his house in a suit and tie. But if he doesn't like the look of ye, you've had it.'

With that pressure weighing on my shoulders, I arrived for tea with the Fletts at the agreed time at their house in Findochty.

Irene was with me. She told me to calm down; no doubt she could see the worry plastered all over my face. The dinner was an intimidating experience to say the least. They were truly friendly people and had prepared an incredibly nice meal for us. We had Jenna with us too, just a wee one-year-old at the time, and she decided to pick this moment to start running around their house. All Irene and I could think was, 'Sit down!' The Fletts had gone to a lot of trouble and I was very anxious to make a good impression. David himself was someone I would describe as a very professional man, genuinely good-hearted, and really I had nothing to worry about. He instantly warmed to Irene and me and could see I was determined to make my way in the world. After tea, he took me to one side for his judgement. Butterflies raced around my stomach.

'So,' he began. 'How does it feel to be the proud new owner of my boat?'

I'd hoped I'd made a good impression. But when he told me

his decision, I near enough exploded inside with delight. Everything I'd worked for condensed into one special moment. I blurted out my thanks, again and again.

I was twenty-six years old.

When I look back across my thirty-five years at sea, and all that I've achieved in that time, I firmly believe that my success was very much down to Mr Flett believing in me. Without that first vote of confidence, all my fiery determination and ambition would not have taken me this far.

There's a little postscript to this story. A few weeks later I went down to Cluny harbour in Buckie, a town located on the Moray Firth coast fifty-five miles to the west of Peterhead, to complete the handover. David Flett was standing by the boat, waiting for me. Before we attended to business, he pulled me over to one side and pointed to a middle-aged man lingering at the other end of the pier.

'Ye see that gentleman over there?' he asked.

I nodded.

'He just offered me forty thousand pounds more than you have offered for the boat,' he continued. Just for a few seconds I thought I had been outbid at the very last moment. Then he smiled. 'If ye want to make a quick buck, go over there and talk to him.' While the thought of making so much money without even stepping aboard the boat was mildly tempting, I politely declined. This boat had been David Flett's baby, and he desperately wanted to see it help someone else get started. Now it was my turn.

Before he sold me the boat, Mr Flett had had her repainted, overhauled the engine, even filled up the tanks with diesel. Basically she was in top, top condition. All I had to do was get ice and food. It was very much, there's the boat, ready for the job, now off you go. You'll hear of some owners selling on boats that are basically done and in need of major repairs. In contrast, the *Seaforth* was kept like a yacht. I was one of the lucky few who could set sail on his first trip out to sea, make a catch, return, sell the fish and put money back into the bank on that same landing. There's not many skippers who can claim to have been so fortunate, and it was all thanks to David Flett.

A skipper's boat is the entirety of his business. If a printer fails in an office it's not a disaster. People can still work. If your boat is not up to scratch then you cannot make money. It is as simple as that. Skippers with new boats and big loans to pay off, especially, simply cannot afford not to bring in a healthy return.

Over the next five years, I never lost a single day's fishing. That boat never, ever let me down.

David Flett himself kept in touch with me for years and years afterwards. While I was a greenhorn lad, he'd been an extremely skilled skipper, at sea all his life, and he used to get very anxious for me. Over the next few years I made some terrible mistakes and did stupid things. In my defence, I had no father with sea experience to guide me. If your dad's a skipper, he might not be on the boat but he'll be on the end of a radio, someone to go to for advice when you sorely need it. I love my father dearly, but he wasn't in a position to help me with fishing matters. David Flett, on the other hand, *did* give me advice – all the time, in fact; but as a young lad, I tended not to heed it, much to my own regret. He once offered to come on a trip with me, to see exactly what I'd been doing wrong. My pride wouldn't allow me to accept.

Years later, when I finally came to sell on the *Amity*, I said to myself, That boat is going to leave me the same way as I got her, in mint condition. I felt it was only the right thing to do. It was like passing on a family heirloom, you wanted to see it treated right, with respect and care.

With the boat now mine, all I needed was a name; it's traditional for a skipper to rename a ship when he takes command of it. I'm not great at names so I entrusted this task to Irene. One night when I was at home waiting to take command of my new venture, I asked Irene, 'Hiv ye thought of a name yet?'

'Not really,' Irene replied. She was busy bathing Jenna. She told me she'd been going through the dictionary, and had managed to get halfway through 'A' before it all became a bit too much, what with a baby girl to take care of and a household to run. She stopped and settled at the word at the very bottom of the page. It was 'Amity'. Happily, the word meant 'friendship' and I thought that summed up perfectly what I wanted to be as a skipper.

'Is that okay?'

'It's perfect,' I said. And it really was.

We never looked back.

The first thing I had to do was get a crew. In those days, finding a crew was never a problem. More of a difficulty was bringing together some guys who worked well together and became a real team, because unity breeds success on the North Sea, and no matter if you were the best skipper in the world, if your crew wasn't up to scratch, you'd be on a hiding to nothing.

A good crew has to find its own level – who gels with who, who's a hard worker, who maybe doesn't give it 110 per cent. For those first few years, my crew had a habit of changing almost weekly; not the entire crew, of course, but one or two guys might come and go at any given time, so much so that the *Amity* sometimes resembled a revolving door as I looked to create the right balance. When I look back now I realise that I had problems with a few guys, but I was just starting out as a skipper and basically glad for anyone. I did, though, consider myself extremely fortunate to luck out with some great crewmen at the beginning of my skipper's journey, none more so than the guy who I hired as my engineer, a Norwegian by the name of Ola. He was a top-notch engineer who could solve almost any problem on the boat single-handed. A skipper's constantly fretting about his boat but with Ola on board, I had no worries about the engine room whatsoever.

Sadly, after six months he left for another boat. Like many

Norwegians, he came from the oil industry, and he'd probably figured on one day returning to it.

That's how it was in the beginning of my career as skipper. A lad might stick about for a year or so before he moved on, then I'd get another guy in to replace him. I discovered two good mates, but the downside to hiring crew members with great promise was that they had the same desire as I had: to own a boat themselves. Both these excellent mates soon followed that path. Others got opportunities to work on newer vessels, a problem I hadn't considered when I invested in the *Amity*.

Although she'd been kept in mint condition, some crewmen – such as the engineer, Ola – would leave for the new boats that were continually being launched from the yard. I was conscious of the fact that my vessel was fifteen years old and didn't have the creature comforts that some guys maybe craved. The *Amity*, for example, featured an outside toilet, meaning you had to leave the main accommodation in the galley and brave the outdoor elements. Not exactly comfortable, though it was better than the previous generation of boats, which came with dry toilets – literally just a bucket that you had to empty overboard.

Water was always in short supply on the *Amity*. Although we were floating on the stuff, we couldn't use any of it. Our supplies were strictly limited to the freshwater we carried on board the ship. The cook was the guy responsible for monitoring the water tank, because he depended on having

At the wheelhouse of *Amity II*.

Taking to the water as we prepare for another trip on the treacherous North Sea.

Peterhead port – the place where every young lad begins his adventure as a fisherman.

Me as a wee baby with my brothers David (to the left) and Peter (in the middle) and my grandfather.

Shooting the nets and hoping all the hard work pays off and a good haul comes at the end of it.

Myself and the crew on a promotional shoot for the BBC series *Trawlermen*. Kevin O'Donnell is to my right.

The crew of *Amity II* taking a welcome break in the galley.

A vessel returning to Peterhead during a storm. You can see how the boat is swaying dramatically from side to side.

Sorting the catch is a key part of prawn fishing. Each and every prawn has to be washed, graded and iced before we land.

Kevin displaying his characteristic good humour. He was great at keeping people's spirits up while at sea.

Mending the nets – a vitally important task and one that every young lad has to master.

Buchanhaven Pier, where I spent a great deal of my childhood, wishing I was out at sea.

The fish market at Peterhead port. This is the moment of truth, where a skipper finds out how good or bad a trip he really had.

At the market with some freshly landed catch. It's the job of my sales agent to get me a good price.

This is where Freddy the prawn ultimately ends up – in a paella dish. Sadly the langoustine is not a delicacy appreciated in many parts of the UK, so our catch mostly ends up on the Continent.

My crew. Bottom row, left to right: Geoff, Jerry, Jonny and Valeris. Top row: Nikolas, Kevin and me.

sufficient supplies to cook us a proper meal. Running out of water – to the cook, that was the biggest disaster in the world, and he'd soon give you a tonguing if he suspected you of wasting it.

The rationing of freshwater meant that wet shaves were out of the question. We operated on a rule of basic hygiene only. On the occasions we managed to utterly deplete our freshwater stocks, we had to resort to unorthodox sources of water. The North Sea itself was out of the question, obviously, but we could rustle up a cup of tea by pilfering icewater from the boxes in the fishroom. Boil it in the kettle and it goes down okay, apart from the filmy scum that forms on the surface of your tea. Still, you can't be too fussy. Fishermen are masters at getting by and making do. Nowadays you have showers on the boats, but the first boats I worked on lacked even that; if you fancied a wash, you had to go on deck and shower using freezing cold, salty seawater.

The *Amity* made up for her somewhat functional toilet in other ways. I actually had my own skipper's cabin, separate from the other beds. Up till then I'd slept in a bunk in the cabin below decks with the other crew; to have my personal space beneath the wheelhouse, equipped with a chart table – I felt this was a great privilege. But the cabin also gave me somewhere to work in peace. The words of the guy on the *Fidelia* during my maiden voyage as skipper – 'On the deck you work from the shoulders down; in the wheelhouse, you work from the shoulders up' – turned out to be prophetic. On a boat, there really is a divide between the skipper and his men, a real me-and-them mentality, and one that I found it hard to adapt to initially.

I'd wander down into the galley and the banter flat stopped. The minute I went back up to the wheelhouse, the conversation started up again. This shouldn't have surprised me, because I did it myself as a deck hand on the *Responsive* and *Fidelia*. The skip's the man, the 'mannie', the *capitano*, the guy upstairs in charge of making decisions that sometimes aren't popular. He's no longer one of the boys. I felt a little bit alone and distant from the lads, but I accepted it as a fact of life at sea and refused to let it bother me.

My first tough call on the *Amity* was sacking a member of my crew.

This particular guy was a bit of a Jack-the-lad. Quite mouthy, he'd made himself popular with the crew. On this occasion we came into port on Saturday to land our catch for the Monday market. The crew had gone home and this guy partied hard over the weekend. He turned up for work on Monday morning with a fair scoot of alcohol in him and he stood on the pier giving it a bit of lip and shouting for the fish to be landed, when the boat wasn't even being prepared for landing. I sacked him there and then. Told him to pack his bags and go. I wasn't proud of this and I hated turning it into a public spectacle, but I had the eyes of my crew on me, as well as the other skippers and crews in port. I had to show them who was in control. I was the boss, and everyone needed to understand that. There's nae place in the world for weak mannies.

The guy came back later in the evening when he'd sobered up, wanting his berth back. I'd already committed myself and wouldn't go back on my decision.

'You want to come down partying and shouting and screaming,' I said, 'you find another boat, because you're not doing it here.'

Although this guy had made himself popular, the crew respected my actions. Now they all knew what I was about.

Like everyone else, I'd graduated to my own boat without having perhaps all the experience I needed for such a demanding role. If I'm honest, I thought at the time that I was ready for the wheelhouse, but in practice maybe I wasn't. Then again, a man's got to go out by himself some day, and you cannot buy experience, so how long was I supposed to wait until I took charge of a vessel? Five, ten, fifteen years? I was hungry to prove myself, and had an unshakeable faith in my ability to survive the occasional setback — or so I reckoned at the time.

In those early days, I definitely made a number of mistakes, and I was conscious of the fact that, by landing catches that were maybe a little smaller than the other boats in the fleet, I was losing the crew money. One of my biggest errors was to do with timing.

When it comes to fishing, timing is vital. Fish go up and down in the sea, depending on time of day and what food is available. In the gloaming and early morning they take to the seabed. At the height of a bright, clear, sunny day they sometimes come up nearer the surface. The timing of where the fish might be influences where a skipper decides to shoot his gear: whether to go for the deeper waters or stay in the shallow areas. I wouldn't call it an exact science, as there's a load of other factors that affect the fish, but you learn about how the quantity of fish changes with time. And you do that by watching others.

The mate's certificate I'd earned educates a guy on how to skipper a vessel. However, it gives him absolutely no instructions about fish, or how to catch them. I had to understand the habits of my prey without any guidance. And that's another reason why, in my last years aboard the *Fidelia*, I continually watched what James was doing. Whenever he shot at a specific location, I'd look at *why* he shot there, taking mental and hand-written notes of his actions.

Despite my shadowing James, though, I still made lots of bad calls early on, such as steaming towards the wrong place, somewhere starved of fish, thinking I was smarter than everybody else in the fleet. My first task of the day was to look at the radar. Multiple boats on the radar was a good sign. Then I'd look out of the window and manually count how many boats were about. In the pre-dawn gloom each boat was no more than a couple of lights bobbing up and down on the sea and I'd identify them by steaming close to each vessel and listening in on the VHF radio. Targets on the radar, lights on the sea ... they were all good signs that you were fishing on a promising patch. On the other hand, getting up and spotting no boats on the radar or the horizon left you with a feeling of dread in your guts. On a few occasions, however, you'll be the only boat in the area and your first haul is a grand one. I'm the king of the fleet right now, you start to think, reaping the benefits of being a lone ranger at sea.

That was what I was hoping for when I explored some unknown fishing ground.

'There's got to be a shoal of fish somewhere,' I kidded myself. Rather than realising, 'Nobody's here because there's nae fish.'

My stubbornness and self-confidence prevented me from admitting defeat at first, but a short while later, with still not a boat in sight, I'd belatedly accept the fact that I'd made the wrong call. Maybe once in a blue moon my gamble paid off, but not often. Only pride stopped me from turning for home the moment that sinking feeling hit my stomach; but eventually I'd remind myself that I was running a business, lick my wounds and head for fresh waters.

With the challenges and mistakes piling up, it was helpful for me to find another skipper in the fleet, a colleague on another boat to share information with. Because when it comes down to it, fishing is all about intelligence. I've had a few trusted friends during my career, and at the time I was seine-netting, I became a close confidant of Sandy Watt, who skippered the *Fruitful Harvest*. We were friends at sea and friends ashore, too; we both had daughters and often went on holiday together, me and Irene and Sandy and his wife Liz. We still do to this day, in fact, that's how much we enjoy each other's company. We had a good relationship because we shared similar lifestyles – he had two daughters, like myself – and, most of all, we shared the same sense of humour, laughed at the same things. We were always up for a bit of fun and joking around, and if something happened, say some unfortunate (but harmless) incident befell a guy ashore, we'd both see the funny side of it and milk the situation for all its worth. We also had a great banter going on between us, and if people didn't know us, they'd take one look at the way we talked to each other and assume we were foes rather than friends. I wouldn't say we had heated discussions, but we took up opposite sides of any debate we had. If Sandy said 'black', I'd say 'white', just because. Or we'd be in a restaurant having a meal and Sandy would get up from the table.

'Now, have a nice life,' he'd say, and walk away. The other guests probably thought we were having a quarrel of some kind, but the banter has been the strength of a friendship that's lasted more than twenty-five years.

The two of us worked less as a pair, but more in tandem, telling one another about how much fish a patch of sea had yielded up for us. A genuine relationship based on honesty and trust was very important – especially after I learned that part of being a good skipper is being a good strategist.

Self-interest rules at sea. I'd find a spot in the North Sea that had a shoal of fish and my first thought was, Aye, there's a good catch to be had here. And my second thought? There's enough for one skipper; not enough for two. And if there's plenty of fish for two, I can guarantee there's definitely not enough for four. If I told someone on the radio about my spot, that skipper inevitably passed the news on to someone else. Word spread like wildfire and before I knew it, twenty vessels rocked up, all trying to fish in that one spot.

I got stung by this turn of events a couple of times. The vast majority of skippers I know are great guys and they'd never go in for the lies and mind-games. However, there were one or two who were perhaps willing to dabble in the dark arts. These guys mastered the technique of being a wee bit liberal with the truth over the radio. One guy might give you a bum steer, and though it went unspoken between you, both you and he knew exactly what he was up to. I can't say I was totally above doing it myself a couple of times. The other guy knew I was perhaps holding something back.

On those few occasions I found myself telling less than the whole truth. Call it a certain amount of truth. I'd never lie to anybody – I don't believe in lying, and I've no time for someone who is dishonest with me. This was, instead, exercising caution over the information I was giving out, and making it more difficult for another skipper to identify the plentiful shoal of fish I'd uncovered, like a treasure buried in the depths of the North Sea. I might, say, deliberately underestimate the amount of fish I'd trawled in a certain area. Down the line, I'd right my tally by moving on to new fishing grounds and making up the difference. This wasn't something I did on a regular basis, after all the sea is open to every fisherman and nobody can lay absolute claim to a particular ground. But sometimes it was a case of, well, if I go blabbing about this the whole fleet'll be descending on here and there won't be any left for me.

Our competitive streaks even coloured the friendship between me and Sandy.

Back when he was actively fishing, Sandy exercised caution around me. I still say to him, to this day, that he never let his guard down upon his return from a trip. We had a genuinely warm friendship ashore, but once we set sail, the dynamics shifted. I stopped being his good friend James and became the opposition, a potential threat to the success of his business. We worked the seas at different times, so when he docked at Peterhead of a Friday night, I'd be getting ready to head out over the weekend. At those times, I found that he was particularly careful about what he said, and to whom. He only released certain information about his trip, keen for me not to work a choice patch of his.

Okay, fair enough, I thought. Speaking as a fellow *capitano*, I could see where Sandy was coming from. He didn't want me to glean all his secrets, because next thing he knows, Jimmy Buchan's hammering up and down on his beat and scooping up the fish.

But I'd then wind up my trip and receive a call from Sandy, discreetly prodding me for the news on my haul. Obviously, Sandy was preparing for his next voyage, and wanting to find out the same information he'd withheld from me.

We were both as bad as one another. I fed him information on a need-to-know basis, and he returned the compliment. That's not to say our friendship didn't exist at sea; of course it did. We still pooled information about other boats, sharing what such-and-such a skipper was doing. Perhaps the competitive rivalry actually made our relationship richer. Me busy sussing out what was in Sandy's brain, frantically trying to find out how much fish he'd *actually* landed through my salesman or another skipper, and where he'd really fished, as opposed to where he said he'd been. I had to source my knowledge through a third party, instead of asking Sandy himself. We both found it part of the fun and camaraderie of fishing.

It's tricky for a skipper to figure out where another ship's enjoyed a good catch, and requires him to think like a detective in order to root out the truth. A guy like Sandy might tow in three or four places during a trip, and perhaps only one of them would bear any fruit. Working it out isn't as simple as looking at a navigation chart, sticking your thumb along Sandy's previous route and saying, 'We'll fish there too.' I had to try and figure it out from talking to him, looking at the catch he'd landed, and putting together the various pieces of the puzzle.

Talking to Sandy on the radio also threw up clues.

I liken radio chatter to reading someone's poker face, except it's more akin to poker voice. Sometimes people stuttered and hummed and errrmed, and you'd think to yourself, 'They're figuring out a wee lie to tell me.' Another giveaway was when they'd avoid directly answering the question.

My approach was always the direct one. Other skippers tried to find out information the subtle way, asking one question that leads to another, trying to be a bit clever about it. I'm the kind of guy that calls a spade a spade, and I'd simply say, 'Where'd ye catch yer fish?'

Sometimes this caught Sandy on the back foot, and from the tone of his voice, as he launched into a reply that skated around the question like a line dancer, I'd know for sure he was selling me an absolute porky-pie. Even today, if I confront him over dinner and say, 'Remember that time ye gave me a bum steer?' he'll let out an uncomfortable laugh. We both know I'm right, but it's part of the game. I never held this personally against Sandy – or anyone else in the fleet. At the end of the day, we're businessmen, and we have to manage our investments as we see fit.

If you know about a lucrative patch, your instincts are to protect it for yourself. And if protecting it means keeping quiet about it rather than announcing the fact to all and sundry, then so be it. I didn't like doing it, and it certainly didn't come natural to me. Had there been some other way around the problem, I'd have taken it. I only held my tongue because I was so desperate for my business to flourish.

The flip side is that it's nae nice to be on the receiving end of a skipper giving you a bum steer. After being sold a few horrible duds, I learned to compare what a skipper told me with what he was doing at sea, where he fished, and what kind of haul he was landing at market. I'd sometimes head down to the market floor myself and look at the guy's catch, because it's possible to tell, on the basis of a skipper's catch, where he actually has been out at sea, as different areas throw up separate species of fish. If I saw a lot of catfish in his boxes, say, I could be fairly sure he'd been shooting his gear around a deepwater edge, maybe near Norway where the continental shelf drops off. I viewed this as a process of gaining knowledge, building up a mental picture of the North Sea in my head.

Irene used to say to me, 'Why are you down at the harbour again? You've only been back ashore for five minutes.'

It wasn't a case of me wanting to be at the fish market, but I simply *had* to be there. The fish market's the place where all the various skippers' lies become reality, and the skippers who've spun the worst ones get found out. Some of the skippers can't help themselves; they're compulsive liars. It got to the point where, if one of them came over the radio, I'd switch it off.

Those same skippers were experts at getting a young buck like myself to explore an area they wanted to try without the risk of losing fishing time in their existing catch spots. They'd manipulate me, planting the seeds in my mind over the radio until I'd be aggressively steaming towards some new spot, thinking it'd bring me a good haul ... and only after I'd suffered two or three disappointments with the nets did it suddenly dawn on me that the other skipper had played fast and loose with the truth. I wasn't overly bitter about this. I'm not sure it's even crookedness, it happens in all walks of life, from the fishing right through to the traders in the money markets.

We spoke in Doric over the radios: pure, unfiltered Doric – the real McCoy. If I wanted to find out who'd enjoyed a good catch, I'd get on to the radio and say, 'Is there a marking there?' Which broadly means, 'Is there a good sign?' Another way of putting it would be to ask if they had a 'guid hallie' – a good haul. If I said, 'There's a guid hallie way a markin o fish through,' that translated as, 'There's a good haul to be had there and a good mix of fish through it.'

The banter, the bum steers, the Doric: we brought all these little reminders of home to the sea. Going to the North Sea is a lonely task. The moment we turned around and set sail for Peterhead harbour, the mood among the crew changed.

By far the toughest part of life at sea was being separated from Irene and the kids for long periods of time. In those days before mobile phones and email existed – today I can reach Irene via the satellite phone – I'd approach port with my heart beating like a snare drum, eagerly anticipating the moment the *Amity*'s ropes were tied to the pier, knowing that Irene would be waiting for me with a whole week's worth of news from friends, colleagues and the other wives. But most importantly, I wanted to see Jenna, with Irene telling me the latest stories about her little antics.

One day I landed at port and came home to find Irene

hopping with excitement. She couldn't wait to get me inside the house, tugging my hand and leading me into the living room. I sat. She plonked Jenna in the middle of the room and encouraged her to say, 'Dad,' her first word. It was one of the proudest moments of my life – seeing my child say that word. Having been away from the family for seven days, unaware that Jenna had started to speak, made that moment all the sweeter.

We had a special ritual for the return home in the Buchan household. I'd come in, take off my shoes, and for the next hour Irene would fill me in on all the latest happenings in everyone's lives over several cups of gulped tea and coffee.

Every five minutes Irene would wriggle her nose.

'Wid ye go and have a shower, Jimmy.'

'In a wee bit,' I'd reply, wanting to catch up on all the fantastic stories Irene was bombarding me with.

We didn't have a shower on the *Amity*. The crew only packed one change of clothes, and even then it was a case of changing only if there was an emergency and you got soaked through in a storm. Other than that, the attire I left the house in – I pretty much returned with the same clobber on, right down to the rank socks that adorned my feet. Naturally, the smell wasn't the kind of thing you'd bottle up and call perfume.

I'd step through the front door with my filthy clothes and a salty beard, and the instant Jenna laid eyes on me I'd chase her round and round the living room, catch her and give her a rub on the cheek with it, Jenna freaking at this monstrous creature, stinking like a fish supper and with a chin like a young cactus.

An hour of the gossip was about the limit before the smell overwhelmed Irene.

'Go and have that shower now, Jimmy, please.'

I'd climb the stairs, my legs sore from a hard shift, thinking, I dinnae smell that bad.

The shower was a huge relief. Lovely hot water, washing away the greasy film of salt and dirt that smothered my face.

Stepping out of the shower, I'd happen upon the bundle of dirty clothes on the floor. As I picked them up, the smell would hit me. Utterly foul. It was as if they'd been marinated in salt, fish, sweat and diesel. Was I actually wearing that stuff in the house? I thought to myself, amazed that Irene could tolerate it for an hour. She must really love me to put up with it!

Into the washing machine the 'aromatic' clothes went.

8

RISK AND REWARD

By the end of the 1980s, I was reaping the benefits of *Amity* and became a proud father for a second time when Amy was born in 1988. Never one to rest on my laurels, in 1989 I switched to pair-trawling with another vessel by the name of the *Rhodella*.

Pair-trawling is where two boats work in tandem. You have two warps attached to a net that's shared between two boats. The vessels keep a quarter of a mile apart, with the net open over that distance. A trawl wire is fixed from the side of one vessel to the side of the other, enabling the boats to remain at a quarter of a mile's length from one another – the wire connects to the net that is being towed between the two vessels.

Each boat tows one warp, and the duties of pair-trawling are shared between the two vessels. One ship sets and hauls the nets, while the other focuses on the towing. The combined pulling power of the two boats means that the skippers can employ a much bigger net, doubling or even tripling your catch. This much more efficient way of trawling means that, when the boats get it right, you can land huge catches of fish such as haddock.

I gained a vast amount of knowledge by working with the *Rhodella*. Her skipper, Malcolm Smith, along with his father Eric, belonged to a well-established fishing lineage. I was very fortunate to be able to pair up with Malcolm. He was a similar age to myself and I enjoyed fishing with him – we were on the same kind of wavelength.

I would say both Smiths played a significant part in injecting some stability into my captaincy. Working in tandem with the *Rhodella* I got a steady crew and together we formed a good pair team, opening up new opportunities for ourselves while a few of the older fisheries perhaps failed to adapt. As a pair-trawler we were catching a load of lemon sole and plaice, high-value species that remained outside the quota system which had been introduced for other species and obviously imposed a limit on what a boat could keep. For several years we did extremely well for ourselves and built up a fine reputation in the fleet.

I had been working flat out on the *Amity* and decided to take a holiday break. The whole family, myself, Irene and our two bairns Jenna and Amy, headed down to Dartmouth in our caravan. It was a lovely break, warm weather and a good chance to recharge my batteries and spend some time away from the boat. That said, I don't like to break off completely from the fishing gossip and I was angling for a way to get my hands on a copy of that week's *Fishing News*.

The *FN* is the must-have paper for all skippers and trawlermen. It's a weekly national publication for the industry and I suppose it's fishing's equivalent of *The Times*. It has all the latest stories on the state of the trade, a classified section with boats for sale and what have you. Ever since the age of twelve, I've not missed a single issue.

I knew the fishing town of Brixham, on the south-eastern corner of the Devon coast, was only about thirty miles away. They were bound to have a copy of that week's *Fishing News*. I thought, if I could get my wife to go to Brixham, I could get to a newsagent's – although obviously I couldn't advertise my intentions to Irene. So I kept badgering her that Brixham would be worth a visit, and eventually she relented.

'Aye, we'll gaun in the morn then,' she said.

Victory!

That night, Irene phoned home to check in with the rest of the family. When she returned from the phone box a few minutes later, she was stonking mad and wearing a scowl.

'A funny thing just happened,' she said. 'Nobody wanted to speak to me on the phone.'

'Aye?' I replied. 'Not your mum?'

'Not mine, and not yours either. The two of them gave me

short shrift. I'm telling ye, one-word answers. "Yes," "No," "Oh-kay." What's that about?'

Both our mums could speak for Scotland and for them to cut Irene short was puzzling. I reckoned they were just busy, told Irene as much, and thought no more about it.

Come the next morning, we hit Brixham. As far as I can remember it was a lovely coastal town, but once I'd popped into the newsagent's I can't say I really took much notice of it. Lo and behold, a copy of the *Fishing News* perched on the bottom shelf. I was chuffed to bits – I had my reading material for the weekend sorted. I paid my money, stashed it in Irene's bag, and went about my day.

We returned to the camp site that night. At last, at the breakfast table on the Saturday, I had a chance to get stuck in to the *FN*. I rubbed my palms, peeled open the first page, flicked through to the centre pages and—

I have it on good word from Irene that the colour drained out of my face. She was left looking at a man with snow for skin.

A small article towards the bottom of the page announced:

THERE WAS ADDED drama at Aberdeen Harbour on Monday when the *Amity* was in a collision with another vessel, sinking it . . .

I was so shocked, I couldn't even force out a word. *Sunk*? I stood up, my legs shaking, reading the words over and over again. Irene asked me what was wrong. Finally, I told her.

'The boat has sunk another boat,' I said.

Both me and Irene went into a mad panic. How had this happened? And why had no one told me? We later found out that my parents had learned the bad news, phoned Irene's parents and said not to tell us, because they knew we'd come straight home. As it stood, I tried to call the offices at the port but it was the weekend and nobody was there to answer my desperate calls. On tenterhooks, eventually I got through to my office manageress at her home.

'I just read the paper,' I said, trying to control my voice. 'Tell me what happened.'

'Don't worry, Jimmy. I can assure you that there's nae damage to *Amity*. In fact, she's back at sea as we speak, fishing.'

I kept saying to myself, There must be some sort of mis-understanding. It's *impossible* to sink a boat and escape without a scratch on your own vessel. However, the manageress was telling the truth. *Amity* had come in to berth and land her catch at Aberdeen while another boat decided to make a run between my boat and the quay. My skipper wasn't focusing so much on what was happening further up the dock, but was trying to berth *Amity*. He'd seen this other boat approaching, but didn't think she was going to try and come between him and the pier. In an attempt to get across the *Amity*'s bow, the boat's skipper gave it full throttle ... the two connected, the sharp nose of my vessel hitting the other right on the shoulder, opening it up like a tin of beans.

Despite my vessel escaping intact, I couldn't stop running

through the drama in my mind, thinking over and over about how close I'd come to losing my boat – and my business. Sadly the owner of the other vessel had lost his boat. I imagine he must have been absolutely devastated; I was pretty upset about the situation, and my vessel was still floating.

Irene saw I was a distracted, anxious wreck and suggested we cut short the holiday. We hooked up the caravan and drove back to Peterhead through the night.

The skipper that day was a guy by the name of Graham Gavin. He'd been my first mate for a number of years and was a memorable character from my days at sea, a really upbeat, positive-thinking guy who wanted to make his way in the world.

Graham had a never-say-die attitude that suited life on a boat, where hardship and obstacles are thrown at a man daily. You cannot be a defeatist type and hope to flourish on the North Sea: keeping your chin up is vital, and this was something Graham excelled at.

We were breaking in new fishing grounds at the time, experimenting with areas on the map that were unfamiliar to us, in order to try and improve our catch and knowledge of the seabed. Skippers sometimes go further afield in search of fish, particularly in the hunt for more lucrative species.

We were confident in ourselves, and ready to take on the challenge of finding new grounds. We towed across bottoms that were a wee bit hard and stony, knowing that they were the choice pieces of ground favoured by the fish. As we grew more sure about our abilities, we trawled into areas of bad ground, pushing our luck to the very limit.

Our daring provided us with some good catches, with a lot of flatfish, plaice and lemon sole: high-value produce that fetched top dollar at the markets. Unfortunately, because our knowledge of the area was limited, we'd sometimes push our luck too far and bring in some bad hauls. I'm not talking just a scarcity of fish – but with our gear torn halfway to shreds too.

A skipper has to deal with two types of torn nets. First, there's nets that are torn to shreds plus fish, which tells you that the tear happened halfway through your trawl. But although you've a problem with your nets, at least you can take some small comfort from the fact you've returned some fish to boost your income. And console yourself with the fact that it could've been worse – the second type of torn nets are the ones damaged without any fish inside them, meaning that you've wasted the last four hours of your trip.

If a net is torn *and* empty, your heart's broken.

When we were trawling new ground, the nets would be severely ripped at least once a week, and often-times twice. This caused us no end of stress. While the nets are damaged, you can't fish, and you're conscious of the fact that the clock is ticking. The crew are anxious about getting a pay, and you're fretting about the mounting cost of your trip and the depressingly empty boxes stashed in the fishroom.

The pressure of mending the nets rests on the shoulders of

the first mate. It's a major part of his job. He's got the skills and the know-how. The importance of mending the nets in double-quick time to shoot another catch means it's a task that cannot be trusted to anyone else.

Sometimes the nets were coming on board in a right state, and Graham's job for the next eighteen hours would be to repair them into working condition; a thankless task at the best of times. He had to fix them up in a tight little corner of the boat with limited space, without the luxury of being able to spread them out on the quay, the boat going from rail to rail in the middle of a choppy sea.

But Graham had the mentality that he'd lie down to nothing. Twenty-four hours after he'd settled down to repair the nets, Graham would open the wheelhouse door.

'Ye'll have to try harder the next time!' he shouted.

That was the cue for me to know that the nets were repaired and once again ready to be shot into the water.

I saw some of myself in Graham, in his determination to build a successful career for himself. Soon he moved on elsewhere to pursue his dream of becoming a skipper. I couldn't blame him for that decision, after all, I'd done exactly the same as him when I decided to leave the *Fidelia*. But that didn't ease the pain of losing a good man. A lot of a mannie's energy goes on assembling his crew, building a sense of purpose and unity among the men below deck, and fighting tooth and nail to hold on to the good ones, because they're powerful hard to come by.

Graham seized his opportunity of skippering another vessel with both hands. He carved out a successful career for himself, emerging as a skipper of some distinction. Sadly, he tragically died of cancer a few years back – a tremendous loss to the Peterhead fleet, and all those men who had the privilege of working alongside him. His life was cut cruelly short, when he should have been in his prime.

Away from the ship, family life gave me great joy. Each time I landed Irene was excited to show me a new word Amy had learned, or a new dance. Absence, they say, makes the heart grow fonder. I'm not sure I agree with that – I was already pretty fond of my two girls and Irene – but I certainly cherished the time I was at home. Spending a significant stretch of my life on water allowed me to appreciate how important my family was. I'd arrive home, sit on the settee chatting to Irene, and Amy would position herself at my feet, listening to me intently.

The two days I lived at home were emotional and precious as pearls. I'd take the girls down to the park, go kite-flying, take remote-controlled cars for a spin. I think I had as much fun as they did! It also felt good to be able to give Irene a break. I'm sure it was a relief for her to get some precious time alone, because while I was at sea, Irene had to take care of the children and run the household by herself.

After those two days, the big moment would come for Daddy to head back to the pier. Seeing me in my work clothes, Amy understood I was leaving once more and grabbed my leg, wrapping her hands around tight, like she didn't ever want to let go. I'd walk down the hallway to the front door, Amy clinging on to my leg, begging me not to go. It doesn't matter how long you've been at sea; leaving your family when you set sail claws at your heart.

I was conscious of the fact that Irene had to work very hard to bring up the children. She was the mum, dad and general caretaker all rolled into one. If the car broke down or the doctor had to be called out in the middle of the night, the responsibility fell on Irene's shoulders. The fact is, for most of Amy and Jenna's upbringing, there was no dad at home. Whether I was there for the girls' first day at school, or to watch them in a pantomime, was down to pot luck and the demands of the fishing. Once you've missed those special days, you're the loser. You cannot retrieve them. They're lost for ever.

Both Irene and I had to make certain sacrifices when I chose the hunter lifestyle. Some of the things that people take for granted – coming home to see their children of a night and at weekends, cosy nights in front of the television with their loved ones. A skipper and his family don't enjoy these luxuries. People say, 'Do you have regrets?' I answer, 'No,' because if you look over your shoulder, you'll find that you're not as unfortunate as many others. I made the decision to be a fisherman, buy a boat and run a business. I haven't regretted it for a moment, even if our family life perhaps seems unusual to most parts of society.

In 1992, Malcolm Smith decided to try something different and went ashore permanently. His father Eric came back full time to skipper the *Rhodella*. Eric's return thrilled every skipper and became the talk of the Blue Toon. He was another skipper who was seen as an Admiral of the Fleet, and the respect he had from his fellow fishermen was eye-opening. For me, it was an honour to pair-trawl with him. A year later, however, Eric decided to sell up, and I saw an excellent chance to buy a very good boat. The *Rhodella* was a newer vessel than the *Amity* and the moment I heard of the Smiths' decision I was in there, thinking, This is it. This could be a smart way for me to buy a newer boat.

I put in a bid for her, not really expecting it to be successful. That's not to say I didn't want to buy the *Rhodella* – I dearly wanted to own her, but I simply reckoned her to be out of my price range. To my surprise, my offer was accepted, and I became the proud owner of a second boat. I decided to call her the *Amenna*, after our daughters Amy and Jenna.

My intention was to sell on the *Amity* and use the profits to buy a newer vessel to solo-fish with instead of pair-trawling. But the timing of my purchase was rank: the fishing industry was undergoing another period of change and the demand for second-hand boats had dried up. My efforts to sell her faltered and I ended up deciding to make the best of the fact I had ownership of two boats, and make my own pair team. Prices for our main catch – haddock – were not as good as they'd been, and now that I'd committed to two vessels, my problems were doubled. I was sure I could make it work, but in order to be successful, I needed a good skipper; someone I could trust to do a good job.

I settled on a guy called John Ritchie. He did a sound job of skippering half of my pair, but the pressure weighed heavily on my shoulders, because now I had to make decisions for two boats; while John was a skipper by name, he took his lead from my instructions. Commanding two pair-trawlers was, without doubt, a period of massive stress in my career. When the going was good, I found the pressure okay to cope with. When I hit a sticky period and things were bad, I had twice the boats, and twice the grief. As for John Ritchie, he quickly came to realise that he had a talent for skippering and could be doing the same job by himself with extra responsibility and greater rewards. He left to purchase his own boat. I realised that, as long as I remained in the pair-trawling business, the other skippers would only ever see the job as a stepping-stone to a standalone position.

I took a long, hard look at myself, wondering where my career was going. The outlook wasn't great. Fish prices were depressed and quotas were becoming a thorny issue in the fleet, so I decided that I'd move into the twin-trawl scene. Instead of two boats hauling one net, twin-trawlers are single vessels hauling two smaller nets, an arrangement that would allow me to target lucrative species like monkfish, cod and langoustines. I gambled that by hunting niche species, I'd get a better return when I landed my catch. I'd noticed that a few boats already in these markets were doing well for themselves.

I say 'decided', but in truth, I didn't have much of a choice when it came to changing my speciality. Opportunities were being denied thanks to directives handed down from Brussels, quota numbers for the amounts of fish we could catch were falling and I could foresee a vast number of difficulties in the whitefish sector in the near future. Those who traditionally caught haddock and cod would find themselves in a right mess. The problems with the quotas were compounded by two devastating decommissioning schemes that wiped out half the Scottish fleet in one fell swoop.

The schemes were a necessary evil, even if I say so myself. The fleet was bloated, and back at port we weren't selling all the fish we had. The catch we did land was sold on for rock-bottom prices. Anyone could've reached the same conclusion that the government did: there were simply too many boats. I don't think the seas would've sustained the intensity of the fishing.

Seeing that the industry was in crisis, the government offered every skipper in the fleet a voluntary decommission. You had to tender to them what you'd be prepared to give up your boat for: £200,000, £100,000, whatever. Because the fishing was so badly over-subscribed, some guys undervalued their vessels in order to make a quick get-out. If you were in dire straits, or perhaps your boat was old and you were thinking about retirement, the schemes were a good solution.

Overnight, fifty per cent of the fleet vanished.

The decommissioning schemes proved one thing: if I hadn't moved across, I'd probably have been gone. What at the time was a gamble proved to be the right thing to do.

I sold the *Amity* to an Irish father-and-son team, Keirin and Finbar O'Driscoll. Although I was looking ahead to a new chapter in my career, I'd grown very attached to the *Amity*. She was my first command and my second love, and it made me sad to bid her goodbye. Now I converted the *Amenna* to twin-trawl. She was kitted out with the appropriate gear and off we went on a new course. I felt excited and ready for a fresh challenge.

Within six months of the conversion, I began to realise the great potential within the twin-trawl fishery. The nets are much smaller, with less height to them, and the higher-value species we were targeting, such as monkfish and prawns, were not covered by the same severe quota restrictions we'd experienced with haddock and cod. The rewards for a healthy catch were tempting. We had targets, of course, but they were far, far bigger; so big, in fact, that I didn't have to obsess over them. I also welcomed aboard a top-class first mate and relief skipper. His name was Geoff Phillips, a Peterhead lad born and bred like myself. In years to come, he'd prove invaluable to me. Geoff would go on to become my longest-serving crew member.

That was the good news. Unfortunately, we were in the market with a converted ship. I've mentioned before about how a purpose-built boat always beats a converted ship hands-down, and that's as true for the *Amenna* as any other. Twin-trawling puts serious demands on a vessel. It's harder on the machinery and harder on the engine. My error was to convert a boat designed for the fairly light fishing of pair-trawling: now the

Amenna laboured under the strain. The fishery was promising, there was plenty of money to be made and all was not yet lost. What I needed, though, was a purpose-built twin-trawl vessel.

Meanwhile, the sea continued to serve up reminders of its powers.

On a calm and sunny day the entry gap to Peterhead port looks big enough to the naked eye, but if you're running there on a storm, it can appear a whole lot smaller. The stress and anxiety is worsened by the fact you're almost home, can even see the lights of the Blue Toon lighting up the horizon. You're so close you can almost touch it, but the harbour mouth in a storm is the final hurdle before you reach the safe haven.

One time we were coming back from a long trip, exhausted and looking forward to our beds. The forecast for the local weather was a south-east gale – the worst possible weather for approaching Peterhead, making the waves run directly into the port. It creates a tremendous pressure, with the might of the whole of the North Sea trying to push in through the narrow harbour mouth. Steering the boat on such a fierce water is a complete nightmare, and you haven't got a lot of room when you're running in. With the sea surging so powerfully, a boat has no choice but to go with the flow. When you start to make your run for port, that's it. Your choice is made and there's no going back.

Not that I was unduly worried. After all, I'd ridden many times into the port during a storm. But when we arrived that morning, the sky and sea was blowing a hoolie, seas running like vast rows of hills. The south-easterly gales always generated more swell, and the *Amenna* rose and dipped like a wine cork in a pan of water.

We were approaching port behind the *Fruitful Bough*, a boat under the command of young James West. Into his first year or two of being skipper, James was captain material from day one, a tremendous young lad who came from a very good fishing stock – both his grandfathers, as well as his father, were extremely successful mannies. It's been my pleasure to work with James down the years, and we continue to work closely to this day.

On this morning, James happened to be running in half a mile in front of me.

I thought there was a real danger of James's boat getting swamped by this giant wave. James could see it too, but he was powerless to do anything about it. The wave continued heading towards him. Even if the wave didn't swamp her, its vast energy might force the *Fruitful Bough* desperately close to the harbour walls, the surge tossing her about. James would have no say in the control of the boat, not when he was up against two hundred tonnes of energy. In those conditions you're going to go wherever the sea takes you, and the reality is that you might hit the walls.

We were speaking to one another on the radio at the time. I asked James a question, and he suddenly went quiet. When I looked ahead through the wheelhouse window, I saw why.

The wave was on top of him. It scooped over the back of

his boat, engulfing it completely. The size of the lump of water and the way it crashed down on top of him were menacing and brutal, the roar so loud it seemed to come from all around us . . . His boat was completely swamped. The moment he got hit, I thought James was gone.

I scrambled on to the radio.

'James, can ye hear me? *James*? Are ye there?'

The *Fruitful Bough* somehow emerged from the sea unscathed, but James still didn't reply on the radio. As we came into the bay, I tried him again.

'James, did ye get a scare just now?'

'Fitya think?' he said, breathing hard. 'Aye, I did.'

The swell shook up James a wee bit, but give credit to the lad, he refused to let himself be cowed by the sea. That morning James experienced what I'd gone through many years before aboard the *Fidelia*, coming face-to-face with the destructive nature of the North Sea. It's a ritual that every fisherman has to confront, sooner or later.

In October 1997, the *Sapphire* sank twelve miles off the coast as it returned to harbour in rough weather. Four men drowned, although the skipper, Victor Robertson, managed to escape through the wheelhouse window before the ship went down.

The government at the time refused to finance the recovery of the bodies. Instead, it was left to the families of the four fishermen to raise around half a million pounds between them to pay for a barge to lift the *Sapphire* up from the seabed.

Understandably, the sinking and raising of the *Sapphire* was a major incident in the town of Peterhead. From our house, overlooking the sea, Irene and I could actually see the area where the boat had been lost. In the weeks after the sinking, the lifting barges arrived and then for three weeks – nothing. A severe gale blew, hampering the barges' efforts to raise the sunken trawler. They could do nothing for the wind, and there was an eerie, haunted feeling about town. It seemed as if the sea really didn't want to relinquish the *Sapphire* and her secrets.

Eventually the weather subsided and we watched as the wreckage of the *Sapphire* was returned to the surface, along with the bodies of the four men who went down with her.

Tragedies like this rock a community to its very core. My heart goes out to the widowed families of the lost men. They have got to go out and somehow live the rest of their lives.

Going out on a trip after a sinking, I was acutely aware that I couldn't let such incidents play on my mind. Of course, they did shake you, and in this instance the crew were all talking about it, with the *Sapphire* having been the focal point of national newspaper and television coverage for the past several days. We were all enormously saddened by it. At the same time, fishermen are hardened to death and loss; this wasn't the second or even the third sinking that had occurred in my time at sea, and you have to try and put it to the back of your mind. We're not painters or office workers. We do a dangerous job in a hazardous environment, and the consequences of that are occasionally tragic. Putting thoughts of lost men or ships to the back of our minds was the only way we could witness something as awful as the loss of the *Sapphire* from the comfort of our own homes and possibly want to take to sea again a few days later. If you went out nervous that the same fate might befall you, well, you wouldn't be concentrating on the job.

The fleet tried to come to terms with the loss of the *Sapphire*. Life gradually returned to normal. We struggled on through adversity, like generations before us in Peterhead.

Early the following year, I got word on the grapevine that an ideal boat was coming on to the market. Her name was the *Ocean Bounty*, and her skipper, Ronald Beagerie, was in the process of building a new boat, hence his decision to sell up. I approached Ronald, offered him a deal that would suit me and suit him equally. In March 1998 I took ownership of the boat and renamed her *Amity II*. Geoff Phillips joined me as first mate and engineer, essentially doing a dual job. He also agreed to become my relief skipper when I went on holiday once or twice a year.

I sold on the *Amenna*; her new skipper converted her back to the seine-net method she had originally been designed for before I purchased her, and she continues to be a successful seine-net trawler to this day. Another example of why a captain should never convert his boat.

9

IFS AND BUTS

Looking back, perhaps I should have taken my first trip with *Amity II* as a sign of things to come.

At the time I agreed a purchase with her owner, the *Amity II* was berthed in Macduff, a small harbour located about forty miles to the west of Peterhead, at a point where the coast gets battered by gales hurtling in from the north. Macduff, like Peterhead was a fishing port, albeit on a smaller scale. It is, today, long since gone. I drove up to the town thinking to myself, This is it. A new boat, a new adventure. Incredible opportunities lay before me.

There's one thing you should know: although I'd purchased the *Amity II*, I'd yet to take the boat out to sea. I'd seen it at the port, of course, but as for steering it along the waters? Afraid not.

Buying a new boat is an art form all by itself. I suppose it's like a driver having to invest in a new car without having the option to take it for a test-drive first. Whether you're making a good purchase or a dud is dependent on your instincts and your ability to spot the tell-tale signs of trouble. A well-maintained vessel, with a high level of general tidiness, working lights, no obvious faults or damaged equipment, is a good indicator that things are okay beneath the hood as well. And the appearance of the skipper is important too.

Skippers and their boats – they're like dogs and their owners. A mannie with an unkempt beard and loose trousers, who doesn't really take care of himself, is unlikely, I'd say, to pay more attention to his ship.

I collected the *Amity II*, feeling good about the boat. Hopping on board, I met the passengers who'd accepted my invitation to join me on her little journey along the coast. My dad, a family friend, and a few other folk. They, too, were looking forward to a gentle bob along the fringes of the North Sea down to Peterhead.

Our troubles began as soon as we left. Those north-east gales had whipped up a fierce swell at the harbour mouth. But nothing could dampen my enthusiasm. I was desperate to get the boat to Peterhead.

There were two rudder controls on the ship: one set in the middle of the wheelhouse, and a second set fixed to the side. Prior to our departure, I'd asked for some work to be done to the controls. As I manoeuvred through Macduff harbour, using the central set of controls, everything seemed to handle perfectly. Upon reaching the port entrance, I wanted to get a better view and moved across to the side of the wheelhouse, where the second set of controls were located. I hadn't navigated out of Macduff before, the swell was making life somewhat difficult for me, and I didn't want to stray towards the abundant rocks either side of the mouth.

I went to steer starboard.

The boat veered to port.

Amity II was heading straight for the rocks.

In the few seconds during which this turmoil unfolded, it struck my mind that I stood a decent chance of crashing my new boat on to the rocks before I'd even got a single trip out of her.

My natural reaction was to come full astern and peel away from the rocks, finishing up broadside in the channel. I scratched my head. What's going on here? I asked myself. The whole ship was acting back to front.

We took stock of the situation and discovered the fault: the engineer who'd replaced the controls had accidentally put them in the wrong way round; now port was starboard, starboard port. The boat was doing the opposite of what I was telling it to do; which explained why we'd lurched dangerously close to the rocks.

Now that I knew the cause of the problem, I was able to get the situation under control, although it's fair to say that my passengers, as well as myself, were given a scare by the boat's haywire control system. I took a deep breath and said, 'Right, it's on to Peterhead we go. Okay?'

It was intended to be a brief trip, but to the guys who weren't professional fishermen and weren't used to the ways of the sea, like my father, it probably felt a lot longer. The North Sea was in a choppy mood that night, rolling this way and that. Such weather had caused me strife in my younger days; I could well imagine how my passengers were feeling, especially my dad, who had a tendency to feel seasick the instant he set foot on deck. I always tell people that the fishing skipped a generation in my family. On a barrelling, rumbling night off the North Sea coast, he suffered every inch of the journey.

The family friend was also feeling pretty wretched. He went to lie down in the galley. I ventured below deck to check on my father. Found him with his arms wrapped around the toilet, looking the worse for wear. A pretty dire sight to say the least.

'We'll be there soon,' I told my father in a vain attempt to reassure him.

A mile off the coast, disaster struck.

The engine stopped.

Unbelievable, I thought. How much bad luck can a boat have on a single trip?

In a situation like this, the skipper's first course of action is to get on the radio and notify the coastguard. The engine dying on me was bad news, but I had a plan of action in my head: contact my shore-based engineer and sort it out over the radio.

'There's nae problem, everybody is safe,' I explained to the coastguard, 'we're en route to Peterhead and our engine has stopped. We're drifting, but we're fine. Repeat, we're all okay.'

'Do you need assistance?' came the hurried reply.

'No, thank you. We'll notify you if we need any help.'

The coastguard, however, seemed especially keen to help in whatever way he could. I think it's great that the emergency services are so quick to respond to distress signals, and I have no wish to disparage a remarkable group of people who risk their lives to save others – but I got the impression the coast-guard that night had spent the last several months itching for some drama and a spot of excitement. Either that, or he must have truly believed we were in a bad way, because he dis-patched both the Macduff and Fraserburgh lifeboats to my aid.

Maroon flares were fired to notify people that the lifeboats were being launched. That night my older brother Peter was teaching at the night school in Fraserburgh. He heard the maroons as they exploded in the sky, but although he knew we were taking the *Amity II* down from Macduff to Peterhead, he simply assumed that it was another boat in difficulty, not Jimmy Buchan on his straightforward jaunt around the coast. It couldn't possibly be Jimmy, he thought. Could it?

We were lying on what's known in the trade as a 'dead ship', drifting along with no power. In extreme cases, dead ships can be battered by strong winds against cliff faces, cutting up the hull like a knife blade through wet paper . . . and sink.

But I didn't panic. If we couldn't get the engine started in the next half-hour, I decided, I'd deploy the anchor, preventing us from drifting towards the cliffs. That, at least, would put the coastguards at ease, because they wouldn't want to have a crew abandoning ship.

I checked on my father again and explained to him that we were drifting aimlessly and some kind of electrical fault was to blame. However, he wasn't in a position to help his son with an electrical failure: my father was not letting go of that toilet.

Amid all this commotion I'd managed to get in contact with an engineer on shore. He verbally instructed me how to rectify the problems. It came down to an issue with the fuel cut-off switch, which needed to be overridden. He told me how to do it, the engine kicked into life, and we were on our merry way again.

Needless to say, when we finally arrived at Peterhead port, my father was quick to get off the boat – the ropes hadn't even been tied to the pier when he leapt over the gap and on to the safety of dry land. He's never asked to come to sea with me since. I wonder why!

Our first trip out fishing hardly fared much better.

In terms of the way it operated, the *Amity II* was totally different to my previous boats. They'd been constructed in the 1970s, when engineering was less advanced. Electrics, pumps – when you lifted up the floorboards it looked like Spaghetti Junction underneath, with pipes snaking in all directions. The *Amity II* was a whole new ball game, and figuring out the workings of it was going to take a considerable amount of time.

I've mentioned previously the workings of bilges aboard a boat and how water builds up within them, and how the excess has to be pumped out on a regular basis. The reason you need to pump out the water is that, if the compartment over-flows, it'll sink the ship.

Amity II's maiden voyage at sea, and we had a major problem.

I couldn't get the bilges to pump properly. Every time I tried to operate them, we seemed to be flooding water in, instead of taking water *out*. We had melting ice in the fish-room, water from the decks, and seawater pumping in. The bilges were close to overflowing.

After a few unsuccessful attempts to correct it, I started to become gravely concerned. If I'd been familiar with the vessel, faulty bilges wouldn't have troubled me. But I didn't know the first thing about the *Amity II*, and my first mate Geoff had to forgo the trip owing to a family bereavement. I was well and truly on my own.

The situation wasn't yet critical, but unless I got the pump working again, I'd be left with no alternative but to take the boat back into Peterhead harbour and suffer the embarrassment of cancelling my maiden trip. I tried the pump a few more times. Nothing. I put in a few calls to shore, and figured out that I'd need to dismantle the pump and inspect the individual pieces. The bilges were nearing a dangerously high level, and I feared that I needed more time to fix the pumps than I currently had. With the clock against me, I began to reconcile myself to heading back home with a faulty boat, an empty fishroom and my tail firmly between my legs.

Help came from the most unlikely of sources: not an engineer, but a classic old salt by the name of Davey Mackenzie. He had sailed with me on the original *Amity* and was now back crewing with me again. A deck hand who had his nose to the grindstone and hands like shoe leather, Davey was in his late fifties and easily the oldest guy in my crew, but what he lacked in youth he made up for in spirit, bringing a positive and upbeat attitude to the table.

Davey could see the concern on my face about my boat and the safety of the crew. I explained to him that I couldn't fix the pump system while the bilges continued to flood; that we were done for and there was nothing for it but to turn around.

'We cannae wait for the pumps to get sorted,' Davey said.

'Fitya propose we do about it?' I asked. A skipper's the top dog, but sometimes it's no bad thing for him to consult with crewmen who've seen as many days at sea as old Davey.

'Bail out,' he replied. 'Ave deen it plenty time before an am nae feirt ti dee it again.'

I thought it was worth a try. The order went down to the crew to start bailing the boat out, using a single bucket on a chain system. The bilges on the *Amity II* are quite substantial, and I had my doubts as to whether, using just one bucket, this was going to succeed. But our situation was desperate and I figured we had nothing to lose. One last chance before heading back.

After tending to some business in the wheelhouse, I went down to the engine room to check on the progress of Davey's bail-out plan. I expected to see Davey at the top of the chain, on the deck, throwing the water overboard. Instead I found him right by the bilge – the oldest man on the boat was nearest to the keel, scooping water out with the bucket and passing it on to the next lad. Up the bucket went, down it came, and the whole process started over again. To see the guys pulling together like that was a humbling sight.

A few hours later, Davey delivered the good news through the wheelhouse window.

'Is that better now, skipper?'

It surely was, I said.

'Aye, 'ave wrung more water out of my socks than you young guns will ever see,' he said as he rolled up another cigarette and headed off back to the galley.

Davey must've seen the relief written across my face. The level of water in the vessel's bilge had subsided to a much safer level, buying me the time to dismantle the pump, check the fault and fix it. Davey's plan had worked. There was no such thing as 'ye can't do' in his vocabulary, and it's people like him who sum up the strengths of our industry: hard-working, practical and ready to muck in and sort out whatever challenge lies in front of them.

I hasten to add that the moment we returned to port, I

went off and purchased a semi-submersible pump so we'd not find ourselves in the same situation in the future. A good skipper accepts mistakes, but only once. Fool me once, shame on the boat. Fool me twice ...

For a few months in 1999, I pair-trawled with James West and his *Fruitful Bough*, and I got to see up close the potential he had as a skipper, despite his youth and relative lack of experience. Working with him gave me a boost; it felt as if I was revisiting my younger days, and I saw flashes of myself in the energy and attitude of James and his crew, who were equally youthful. I think me and the guys on the *Amity II* must've looked like grandads to them. In my earlier days, I'd been haphazard, up for a challenge and willing to improvise if I wasn't sure what to do in a particular situation. James was the same.

During one trip, we happened to bring in a massive haul that turned out to be a giant rock. We call rocks 'Mini Coopers' in the industry, owing to their size. This rock, however, looked more like a saloon car. It was so large, in fact, that James was unable to haul it aboard his ship. We now had a problem. Until we managed to dislodge the rock, no more fishing could be done.

The beauty of pair-trawling is that you work together, so if something goes wrong, help is immediately at hand. Seeing James struggle with the rock, I offered to give it a go with my winch, which was bigger and capable of handling heavier lifts.

The North Sea that day was flat and calm as a mill pond. I

gently navigated the *Amity II* towards James, manoeuvring until we were within touching distance. Grabbing the net with my winch, I began to retrieve it over to my side . . . and soon found myself in difficulty. The rock was so heavy it forced *Amity II* and the *Fruitful Bough* to slowly glide together, each boat pulling up half of it.

I heard a gentle *bang*, laid my eyes on the deck, and found that the rock's weight had firmly berthed the *Amity II* alongside James's vessel. We needed to get the rock fully across, by hook or by crook. At this point, James and his crew stepped over from his boat to ours to assist in bringing over the boulder. For a few moments, the *Amity II* had a twelve-man crew and the *Fruitful Bough* was as empty as a ghost town.

'Fitya dee'in'?' I said in mock horror.

'Giving ye a helping hand,' James cracked. We were laughing at his empty boat, not a man left on to steer it, as if the crew had abandoned ship and slunk off to the pub. Because of the way the pair-net directly connected the two boats, we weren't at risk of drifting apart. But still, seeing an entire crew hop from one boat to the next, while their own ship bobbed along like a car left with its doors open in the middle of the road, has to go down as one of the more unusual sights of my career at sea.

I built up a great relationship with James from then on. We gave each other nicknames. James being a thin, slightly built kind of guy, I labelled him 'lamb chop', as there's not a whole lot of eating on him. Whereas James refers to me as 'T-Bone'.

I guess I've got a wee bit more meat on me. And that's the secret to the fishing. A skipper can be as talented and hard-working as he likes, but he also needs to enjoy it. I've always endeavoured to fish with a smile on my face, and it's easier to get on with the job when you're having good banter with a guy like James.

Pair-trawling with James was good fun – on the surface. But underneath, I frequently worried about *Amity II*. She was developing problems. Serious problems. The kind that, if I didn't manage to fix them, had the potential to derail my business, bankrupt me and wreck my life as a skipper for ever.

My two previous boats had been the pride of the fleet when I'd purchased them. The *Ocean Bounty* was a big box of steel, nearly ten years old, and had a lot of things wrong with her. I'm not saying the skipper knew she had these problems, but the fact is they were there. She had propulsion gearbox issues and engine difficulties that, in my opinion, were perhaps down to the age of the boat more than anything else. It's perfectly possible that the boat served the previous owner well while, unbeknown to him, storing up problems deep in its belly that only came to light when I took ownership.

We weren't despondent – not to begin with, anyway. I could see potential in the boat in those times when we succeeded in getting her fishing, returning a big catch with no quotas and a good feeling about the crew. But more often than not she was docked for repairs. We were losing earnings as she wasn't fishing and we had to add the cost of repairs on top of that. For the first two years, the bank loan went up and up, and I felt badly frustrated. Here was a high-value, quota-free market, and a boat that theoretically had the horsepower and setup to make the most of the opportunity in front of me, and yet every time she steamed out of Peterhead port, I wasn't confident that she'd survive for the duration of the trip. I just didn't know what she was going to do next. It got to the point where I found myself losing faith in her.

We'd stop to repair some damage to the gearbox. Head back out to sea and if we were lucky, maybe get a couple of trips without any trouble. Then we'd find that there was a problem at the front-end of the engine, where the hydraulics were driven from. So we'd have to dock again and spend two or three weeks waiting for those repairs to be completed. Back at sea again. Two or three trips later, something would fall off the engine. I remember one particular time, we were merrily towing away when the fuel pump fell off, just like that. Let me tell you, fuel pumps aren't designed to fall off engines.

A year after I'd purchased the vessel, it felt as if everything was going wrong – and I mean *everything*. I'd sunk further and further into debt, the problems were continual and I thought to myself, this could destroy the little empire that I'd so carefully strived to build.

I felt pressure as I had a huge loan to service from the bank; and from my crew, who I had to give a pay even when the *Amity II* broke down. On certain days it seemed as though my head was trapped in a vice, crushing me. I thought that I was reaching breaking point.

The boat's problems were jumping from one end to the other. *Amity's* engine has hydraulics at the front and propulsion machinery at the back, and we were constantly on tenterhooks as to which part would choke next. We'd discover that the engine needed new cam shafts one week, and a few weeks later, another problem cropped up and we were back to square one.

It seemed like I was trapped in a nightmare. One time the boat flooded while she was docked in the harbour and sank halfway, up over the engine with water. I hadn't been down to see her for a couple of days and when I heard the news, I hit an all-time low. How much more of this can I take? I secretly wondered.

When you've got mounting problems, silly things start going through your head. A voice inside me said, Maybe you should just cut and run.

The day the *Amity II* sank, I sat in the engineer's office while she had her engine flushed out and the oil washed out of her, desperately trying to get her prepared for sea. An engineer based at the port, a young apprentice, came through the door, clutching a filter. Standing in front of me, he reached a hand into the filter and pulled out a handful of metal filings. I looked at these splinters of dark, smashed-up metal and, not quite believing they were from the *Amity II*, said: 'Whatever boat ye were working on, loon, you'd best gaun and tell the skipper he's got a serious problem on his hands.'

The engineer looked back at me, black grease smeared across his face, as if he'd popped his head up a chimney.

'Jimmy, this is from yer boat.'

Even though I'd endured my fair share of problems, I refused to believe that my boat was chewing up machinery inside. When those words came out of the engineer's mouth, they floored me. Not only had I to cope with the news that the *Amity II* had sunk and suffered a load of water damage, but now I had a gearbox that was ready to smash up added to the list of problems.

All the while my stress levels went through the roof. Irene saw the changes in me during my days at home. My body language was different. I was irritable and unusually quiet. She told me I was losing faith and blaming everything under the sun for my difficulties with the boat. That's what happens when you're faced with a fiasco: you tend to blame everyone for your problems. Everyone else, that is, everyone except for yourself. One day, Irene sat me down at the table and looked me in the eye.

'Ken, I know we've got all these problems with the boat. I can see that. But at the end of the day, you're the guy that skippers this boat. She's proved she can catch fish – she was successful in the past, aye?'

'Aye,' I replied.

'Then it's nae the boat,' she went on, shaking her head. 'It's nae the nets. It's you.' She paused, letting the words sink in. 'The problem is you, Jimmy. Your attitude. You've got to get this . . .' she searched for the right word, found it, '*defeatist* attitude out of ye.'

I nodded. Sometimes you can't see the forest for the trees, and you need a strong woman to cut to the chase.

'More so,' Irene said, 'if ye go down to the boat with an attitude like that, what's the crew gaun think? If you've lost faith, Jimmy, the crew's gaun lose faith too.'

I was full of 'ifs' and 'buts', but Irene never wavered until her point was hammered home. I was the guy in charge of the *Amity II*. I was the one who had the ability to dig us out of this hole. Nobody else could do it. Either I bucked up my ideas or let my dreams go to waste. By this time I'd been a skipper for seventeen years; I'd proved time and again that I could catch fish, and plenty of them at that. And there was fish to be had out there – one look at the other boats in the fleet told you that they were doing well.

Owning a boat is like a marriage: you've got to work at it from both sides. That vessel tested me to the limits, and I think that, in some ways, I was lucky to buy such a troublesome ship. When you're in a hole, you have to learn that you cannot go around forever coming up with excuses for this and that. The only way out of that hole is to stop feeling sorry for yourself and get busy climbing. And I could moan day and night, and accept my lot as a guy who used to be a top skipper, or I could fight. After Irene's pep talk I doubled my efforts to be optimistic around the crew.

When things seem to be working against you, losing faith is the easiest thing in the world to do. I'd had a lot of knockbacks with the boat, it had dented my confidence and professional pride; I'd gone from being a decent fisherman to one who wasn't making a living, and that's a hard fact for a guy to swallow.

I'd become fixated on the boat's problems, without trying to think logically about how to get beyond them. You have to take the blows on the chin, get on with it, and think, okay, we sort this out and that'll be the end of my problems. Then you can concentrate on making the boat work and reaping the rewards. It sounds simple, but pressure is brilliant at making you blind to the positives in life. If you're up against it, you slide into a depressed mindset, focusing on the negatives. I'm a forward-thinking, optimistic guy, but that boat came perilously close to defeating me.

Two years into my ownership of the boat, and we still had serious problems. The engine was constantly vibrating whenever we were at sea, and pinpointing exactly what was causing it proved beyond us. The engineers at port admitted they'd never seen anything like this before.

Finally, it got to the point where I decided to call in a specialist. My whole life savings were tied up in this business. *Amity II* had cost me over £300,000 in bank loans I wasn't in a position to service, which meant the interest was increasing, and I was watching everything I'd ever worked for slip away before my very eyes. Up till now my career had been on a fairly successful trajectory. I'd had a few hiccups, but nothing on the scale of what confronted me now. In my darkest moments I feared that the boat was going to destroy me.

We knew that the sheer wealth of problems the boat suffered from meant that something was seriously wrong, and patching her up each time she broke down was no long-term solution to our problems. The specialist, I prayed, would sort the *Amity II* out once and for all. The guy was an analyst in torsional vibration, which focuses on the crankshafts in engines. He didn't come cheap, but he had been involved in vibration work his entire life. If anyone could fix my vessel, it was him.

He came on board, went down to the engine room, switched on his vibration equipment and a few seconds later looked up at me and slowly shook his head.

'There is a major, major problem in this vessel,' he said, confirming my worst nightmare. I wrung my hands. 'I'm talking *serious*, Jimmy.'

'Fit we gaun do?' my mate asked.

'I'll speak to the insurers,' I said.

I set up a meeting with the insurance company. This was make or break. Either they helped me out with the cash, or the boat was never going to be fit to sail. I went to that meeting determined to get the result I needed, and after the pleasantries I came straight out with it.

'Look,' I said, 'some of these problems we've had so far with the boat, we're already claiming damage on, and it surely can't continue like this. You've got to help me out with the repairs and fix the boat for good, not just papering over the cracks.'

'That's all well and good,' the insurer replied, 'and I do

understand where you're coming from.' He sighed. 'But the truth is, Mr Buchan, we can only pay *on damage*. We cannae pay insurance out on an assumption. And that's what you've got here, Mr Buchan. An assumption. We'd need hard evidence before we agreed to help you out here.'

What they were telling me was, in effect, that until something actually broke, the insurers were unwilling to cover repairs. The vibration analyst might have found the core of the problem, but they weren't happy to foot the bill. I started to think that I'd hit a brick wall. That there was no way back for me.

At that point Scott Allen, the analyst, who was in attendance with me, stood up, pointing his finger at the desk, and said, 'If you open up that engine, the figures that I am seeing are so bad – so, so bad – this vessel is gaun for a fatal failure, and ye'll have all the evidence you need to make the claim.'

Well, I thought. This is all I need to hear.

But Scott's words must have done the trick, because the insurers agreed that they would pop along for an inspection of the boat. I suppose Scott's doomsday speech put the fear into them that it might never work again.

I phoned up the manufacturers and said to them, 'Right, there's a problem in the engine and we need you guys to open her up.' The engine could only be got at by the manufacturers, so their support was vital. They came down and opened up the front of the engine, exposing the crankshaft. Me, my crew, Scott and the insurers huddled around, my heart beating so hard I could feel the throb of it in my hands and feet. Inside the belly of the *Amity II*, we saw the full horror.

The crankshaft was cracked. Ready to smash. I was stunned, as were the insurers. The only guy who wasn't surprised was Scott. His figures had already told him the truth. The engine was literally worthless.

Had the vessel continued to fish, in that state, the consequences could have been catastrophic. Maybe the engine would fail coming into port on a stormy night. No doubt about it, bringing in Scott had been the right decision at the right time. Oddly, seeing the battered crankshaft didn't make me despondent; I felt the opposite, in fact. The weight lifted from my shoulders, because now, for the first time since I took ownership of the *Amity II*, I could see a future with her. What I was looking at wasn't pretty, but it did seem to me like the end of her problems. Replace this crankshaft and she'd be raring to go. The only downside was that repairing the engine was going to cost a lot of money.

To be fair, once they'd had sight of the engine, the insurers agreed to help me out. We plumped for a completely new system, renewing the gearbox, the engine and the hydraulics. The way boats work, all these parts are intermingled and the only way of guaranteeing that there'd be no further problems down the line was to rip everything out and build from scratch. We left no stone unturned, nothing to chance. When that boat went back into the water, I didn't want any more hitches.

The insurers said they'd restrict their payout to consequential damages, and some of the repairs didn't fall into that category. But at least they helped ease the burden. I didn't exactly have a lot of wiggle room with the bank by this point. The repairs came to £200,000.

Perhaps I should've been elated once the boat was deemed to be in a seaworthy condition. But in the back of my mind was the realisation that the amount of money I'd borrowed had skyrocketed in the two years since I purchased her. I'd added another £250,000 to my original loan, and if I didn't start raking in money, and quick, I'd soon end up bust.

In hindsight I suppose I could've walked away from the boat once the full scale of the engine problems was revealed. Tried to sell the business on and given up on my dream. Or, I could gamble everything I had and then some. Strive with every sinew to make it work. I'm not a perfect man and have certainly made my fair share of mistakes. But I've never, ever been a quitter.

On my first trip back out aboard the repaired *Amity II*, I had nothing to blame. The engine was good, the hydraulics were good, the gearbox was good. The fishing gear was good. The only person responsible for any mishaps was the skipper: me. I knew then that, with no excuses in easy reach, I had to pit my will against the sea, plain and simple.

Life wasn't suddenly a bed of roses. I had a lot of debt to service, including the extra load I'd shelled out for the new engine and equipment. We'd lost a great deal of fishing time and had to make up ground on our colleagues in the fleet.

Now, however, there was a light at the end of the tunnel. I could look ahead with hope.

That was the most dire period I'd ever experienced. My career – my *life* – could've veered off in a radically different direction, had it not been for a strong family, an iron will and Irene and Geoff. There's a few people that might not admit to such a thing, but I'm proud to say that it took a good woman to put me on the straight and narrow.

Now I could get on with the business of hunting prawns. I quickly learned it was a twenty-four-hour slog, and unlike any challenge I'd ever faced at sea.

Prawns, sometimes known by their French name, lan-goustines, are highly prized on the Continent but not really a feature of menus in Britain. It's an example of the lack of a love affair in the UK with seafood, and it saddens me that such a large proportion of this wonderful produce ends up on dinner plates in France and Spain.

When we went into the prawn fishery with *Amity II*, me and my crew were fairly new to the concept. We'd caught lan-goustine before, but it had never formed the bulk of our catch. Now we found ourselves in a position where the blind were leading the blind. We were doing what we thought was right, but getting only a modest return. Each time we went to market we came away thinking, Maybe we'll do better next week.

Prawns live hundreds of feet below the sea surface,

burrowed away in tiny mudholes. They give you no rest. They don't behave like fish, grouping together in fat shoals that you can trap in one fell swoop. Prawns are spread out across the seabed, so you've got to cover ground fast and wide to scoop them up.

I might trawl down a stretch of fishing ground one day, and not pick up enough prawns to feed the cat. Trawl down the same stretch the next morning, however, and I'd collect a big haul. The mudholes that prawns live in sometimes reach depths of up to two feet, and it's only when the creatures pop their heads out of the mud that you get a catch. But when they burrow out of their holes, boy do they come out in numbers. There's no rhyme nor reason to their behaviour, and it's not even about skill. I needed patience when it came to this fishery. Patience, and a good nose for fishing grounds. The thrill of snaring the prawns spurred me on.

A returned catch of nephrops, to give the prawns their scientific name, is a highly unusual sight. The nets bring up all kinds of creatures, from heavily armoured spider crabs and tiny hermit crabs to large whelks: all these creatures are protected by some kind of spiked-up, hard outer shell. And I think to myself, Boy. It must be absolute war down on the seabed. Why else would every type of life down there need to be sporting armour?

Another difference between trawling for whitefish on the original *Amity* and hunting the prawns on *Amity II* was the continuity of the fishing. We had a lot of highs and lows in the whitefish trade; we worked with volatile markets where the price was set on the spot by the merchants. Sometimes the prices were very good and we'd get a huge return on our catch. Other times, we'd come in, find the prices depressed and the return would be bad.

The prawn industry is based on contract price. There's no auction. When I docked the *Amity II* and my catch was unloaded, my prawns were taken to the factory and weighed and graded, and I got paid according to weight. That made my life much easier; with every box we filled, I was able to work out how valuable my catch was. It also made the prawns a much steadier fishery, allowing me to look ahead and think, Okay, I'll have this creditor paid off in two months and that one in three. With a steady flow of cash and a happy crew getting a good pay, over the next two years I was able to crawl out of the debt I was in.

I felt my confidence soar. With the *Amity II* back on the road, nothing could stop me. When I did suffer the odd poor haul, I was able to take it on the chin and move on to the next trip. I'd say to myself, well, it's nothing I've done wrong, it's just Mother Nature. Prawns aren't out this week, bad weather or big tides, forget about it. There's always next week.

My biggest concern was always my crew. I've said before about how my crew and I were in a me-and-them situation, but that's not altogether true. They were very much like me, in that they needed to earn money, and I felt a big responsibility to give them a good pay at the end of each trip.

One knock-on effect of switching fisheries was the need to maintain the quality of the catch. Long ago, I'd happily scoop up as much fish as possible, keep it in fairly good condition and bring it in to market. But the way to handle prawns was very different and it took me a small while to figure it out. I had one especially bad trip where my fish agent made me see the light, and changed the way I've handled my catch ever since.

This bad trip was an eye-opener. Twenty-five per cent of the prawns went to waste. Of course, every skipper gets an element of waste in his catch, but he's looking for two or three per cent. If I get five per cent waste nowadays, I view that as a bad trip. So for *twenty-five per cent*, I knew automatically that we were doing something seriously wrong. What I had neglected to realise was that, in this new fishery, we needed to manage the catch with much more attention.

Distraught about the bad catch, I went and spoke to the factory manager. It's my belief that when you're in difficulty, the worst thing you can do is switch off and pretend you're not in trouble. It's your responsibility to find out what you're doing wrong and make sure it doesn't happen again. The factory guys gave me advice on how to ice and wash the langoustines, as well as suggesting some other ways we could improve quality control. I also had a chat with some seafish specialists. They carried out an analysis of the production on my boat and recommended some radical changes to the way we did business. The grading and washing of the catch had to be done properly, and we had to rapidly chill the prawns. This was especially a problem in summer, when the catch came out of the sea at between 12 and 14°C. The minute we washed the prawns, we put them in a chilled bath for five minutes to lower the temperature as quickly as possible prior to loading them into the fish boxes.

Now, instead of piling the fish high and hoping for the best, my aim was to improve the quality of my catch. But you cannot achieve anything without convincing the crew to accept your way of doing things. I'm a skipper, but that doesn't necessarily mean the men below deck follow my orders to the dot, which is why I think you've got to be a good communicator and a people person. It's no use saying, 'Do it this way,' and leaving it at that. You have to emphasise to the guys that it's in their interest to maintain the quality of the catch. If they don't, under the share system, they all stand to lose out.

I still find nowadays that I'll get the odd bad catch. The processor will call me up and say, 'We got a problem this week, Jimmy.' I put those catches down to production drift – a change of crew where someone has joined the *Amity II* and thought to themselves, I'll just do it my way. When that happens, I've got to go out and hammer it home to the lad that he can forget how he's maybe done it on another boat – there's only one way with me, the *Amity*'s way. That's also where the mate comes in handy, because I can't be everywhere all at the same time. If I'm in the wheelhouse, I'm not seeing for myself how the crew are handling the catch, and the mate is my eyes and ears, feeding back to me any problems.

In 2007 my on-shore commitments increased, when I accepted the role of Chairman of the Scottish Fishermen's Organisation after serving as a director for twenty years. I was obliged to take time off to attend meetings and work with industry associates, and I spied an opportunity to show my appreciation by essentially job-sharing with Geoff. It was a chance to show some sort of payback for his loyal service: if I didn't use Geoff's skippering skills, some other skipper might. All in all, it made sense for me to have Geoff as a relief skipper, running the boat when I was tied up with other business.

These were good days, the catches were steady and the crew a happy bunch. There were periods when the going wasn't so great, of course, but that's a fisherman's lot: no two days are ever the same, no two trips. He has to respond to new challenges and dramas every time.

Owning a boat is like inviting your life to be a series of highs and lows, and I suppose that's why skippers, like their farmer counterparts on land, are seen as being typically a bit cynical and jaded. I try to be more cheerful than that – I hope, anyway – but I see where they're coming from. When the going's good, it's the skipper's responsibility to keep everything in perspective. But the opposite is also true: when he's in a slump, or disaster strikes, he's got to be the one geeing up his crew and remaining optimistic in the face of some monumental challenges.

A skipper also needs a good first mate. And there was only one person refused to ever slip into a mire of defeatism: Geoff.

He was a big source of support during the most testing period of my career, constantly geeing me up and telling me that we'd be out of this rut eventually. More than that, he always found a way to patch up the boat when she failed, so that we could sneak in an extra couple of days' fishing. When we did manage to get to sea, Geoff's ability to keep the *Amity II* ticking over allowed me to get the crew a pay.

I can honestly say, hand on heart, that had Geoff gone, I probably would have been finished as a skipper. He was instrumental in me keeping my sanity. Geoff was the most loyal guy I'd had the privilege of working with, he kept morale up with the crew and was a sure hand at the tiller in the face of a sorely testing situation. Even when guys I'd employed sought out berths on other boats, Geoff brought stability to the crew – and to a situation that was critical.

Geoff has been a rock for me down the years. As first mate he provided a conduit between me and the rest of the crew. Quiet and unassuming, without any airs or graces about him, Geoff didn't give the impression of being a ruthless ruler. Instead, he achieved results through respect. He respected the crew, because he excelled at bringing the best out of people. That encouraged the guys, in turn, to respect Geoff.

He's not an aggressive guy but he has a shrewd mind and doesn't suffer fools gladly. If you're willing to learn, and have the desire to earn an honest buck, Geoff's a great teacher, and will pass on to you the skills he's accrued down the years. Timewasters, on the other hand, need not apply.

No matter what, I can never truly repay Geoff for the loyalty he showed me in those miserable days. He could've easily looked at the boat, thought to himself, 'Well, this is a pile of rubbish,' and moved on to pastures new. Geoff wouldn't have been short of offers either: he's such a good hand, and word of mouth passes quickly around the port.

Geoff worked well with me, and he'd perfected the skills necessary to be a top-class first mate. But I also appreciated the fact that he fitted into my system and bought into my vision of how I wanted to work the fishing.

My style of management is fair and friendly, but there are certain lines that can't be crossed, and I expect the crew to carry out my wishes without question. Geoff slotted into that setup perfectly. I passed my orders down to Geoff, and he was charged with then ensuring that the guys below deck did what I'd asked of them. The first mate's job can be tricky. Being the conduit between the captain and the crew, and he's on the receiving end should a guy have a beef with my decision-making.

On one occasion I happened to be passing the galley while Geoff addressed the guys. As he instructed the crew on the next job, one smart alec stepped forward, an angry look in his eyes. The look of a man intent on causing trouble.

'I dinnae agree with this,' the guy said. 'We should do it in anither way.'

My neck muscles tensed. I could see a confrontation stewing. I might have to intervene, I thought, before this gets out of hand.

I hadn't counted on Geoff. He went eye-to-eye with the smart alec. Calmly looked him in the eye, the rest of the crew watching this showdown unfold, me on the sidelines and ready to back Geoff up.

'I'm the mate,' Geoff said in a stern but reasoning voice. 'But—'

'Nae buts. This is fit we shall do.' The smart alec held Geoff's stare. 'Even if it's wrong. Ye ken?'

A silence hung over the whole crew. This goes one way or the other, I thought. Either he punches Geoff, or he backs down.

'I said, ye ken?' Geoff repeated.

'Aye,' the guy finally replied. He averted his gaze. Backed down, and knuckled down with the job, muttering under his breath. Geoff had laid down the law and called the crewman's bluff. And he'd won.

Geoff was a stand-up guy, ready to put his neck on the line – but then again, perhaps he could afford to do that, because he was rarely, if ever, wrong.

He knew his position on the boat handed him responsibility for some of the operations, and he emphasised to the crew that it was his place to make decisions, not theirs. Like me, Geoff believed that it's crucial to project a confident manner, even when things aren't exactly going according to plan.

I recall one time we were heaving the nets up. A wise guy stood to one side, chippering away and moaning just loud enough for Geoff to hear him above the grind of the stuttering machinery. The guy was complaining about this, that and the other. Soon as he heard the crewman, Geoff brought the machinery to a crashing halt.

Everyone stopped what they were doing. Eyes turned to Geoff and the wise guy.

'Look here,' he said, 'this is how we're gaun do it, and I don't care whether you like it or not.'

The wise guy tried to look away, but Geoff kept on at him, his voice steady as granite. 'You can disagree till yer blue in the face, but all that matters is that I'm the first mate. And this is how I want to do it.' A chill silence cut through the air. Some of the crew looked at their feet, shifted awkwardly. 'Now keep heaving.'

The guy quickly zipped his mouth shut. Crisis averted. We didn't have another peep from him for the remainder of the night.

Respecting the chain of command is just as important to the success of a boat as the condition of the vessel and the abilities of the crew. If there's something I specifically wanted done, I put it down through the chain of command to Geoff. Whatever I said to Geoff, whether he thought my instructions were good or bad, he'd not say a word, because of the respect he had for me. The old truism is that the skipper's never wrong.

Of course, I shared the same level of respect for Geoff, and sometimes I'd ask for his input.

'Fit do ye think?'

And Geoff would pipe up with, 'Well, I think this . . .'

But he'd only speak his mind once I'd invited the question.

To those who've not worked at sea, the chain of command might seem a bit rigid for a fishing trawler with four or five guys aboard. It's nae the Royal Navy, you might say. And you'd be spot on. However, there are times when you absolutely need to rely on the chain to maintain discipline on your ship. This is especially true when it comes to having troublesome crew members.

The North Sea does funny things to a man. I've seen more than a few guys turn once the boat leaves the comfort of the port. Perhaps a guy's having issues in his personal life, or dealing with a financial burden that plays havoc on his mind. Whatever the reason, the tension builds in him. Nothing appears to be wrong on the surface, but he's boiling up with resentment inside. Three days into a trip and a succession of bad hauls, the guy's been out on watch in a foul night, cold rain lashing down on him like needle points, he's got by on two or three hours' sleep for the last couple of nights, and I've asked him to carry out a task he's perhaps not comfortable doing.

His safety-valve snaps.

At that point, Geoff steps in. He'll take the guy aside and firmly remind him of the number one rule of a fisherman's life. 'The skipper's word is final.'

Inevitably, you get guys who think they know better than the captain. If they smell weakness, they'll pounce and try to rule the roost. Geoff, as the first mate, was tasked with nipping these troublemakers in the bud before they got out of hand,

and reminding them of who the leader was at sea. Once the guys are aware of the chain of command, it's much easier to get down to the business of catching fish.

Still, nobody's perfect. I have to make a lot of decisions on the spot, and although you might have thirty-odd years of experience and the instincts of a hunter, you'll still get decisions wrong every now and then. It's important you don't let those bad calls turn into widespread dissent among the crew.

Skippers have lost control of their boats in the past. I wouldn't call them mutinies, but you'd get a new, fairly inexperienced skipper taking his boat out, only to find his crew refusing to perform their duties once at sea. For me, that's less to do with the skipper's abilities than with creating a situation where the first mate doesn't have control of the crew, so every man below deck thinks he's in charge. These guys had to return to port, ashen-faced at the crew's protest. What it highlights is how you've got to be decisive at sea. You can't be seen to ponder about. Showing you're in control of the situation, even when you're not, is vital. My advice for anyone wanting to captain a vessel is this: Look confident, talk confident, and never show any self-doubt.

Of course, some guys in a crew are easier to handle than others. There's a bad apple in every barrel, so the old saying goes, and the same is true for crewmen. Luckily, most of the guys aboard the *Amity* and *Amity II* have been a pleasure to work with. Genuinely lovely people. One chap, however, was the proverbial bad apple.

I offered him a berth several years ago. A skipper has to hire and fire by gut instinct, because he's only seeing the guy ashore, in a totally different working environment. It never occurred to me back then, however, that a man's personality could change so dramatically from dry land to the sea.

My first impressions of this guy were totally positive. He came across as decent to a fault, willing to please, and he seemed to possess knowledge and depth of understanding of the job. All in all, he appeared the perfect guy for my crew. I hired him on the spot.

Trouble began a mere six hours after leaving port. His personality changed, as if someone had thrown a switch in his brain. The first warning sign was his aggressive behaviour. Most new berths are really quiet for the first few days at sea. They don't know the crew and the boat's unfamiliar; it takes time for a man to feel his way into an environment, until the bunk becomes his own and the other guys are his new best friends.

This guy, on the other hand, immediately started to try and take control of the ship, ordering the rest of the crew around, telling them how he did things differently to us and generally making a nuisance of himself. Wow, I thought, this guy's a weird one. It wasn't the first time I'd witnessed someone flip, but he was by far the most extreme case.

Alarm bells rang. I pulled Geoff to one side.

'We might have a wee problem on our hands here,' I said.

Geoff nodded. He'd seen the guy acting out of order.

'I'm on guard for him. He might need a reminder that there's only room for one captain on the boat.'

Forty-eight hours into our trip and I wasn't enjoying a great deal of luck with our hauls. Our returns weren't disastrous, but neither were they anything to write home about. This guy took it upon himself to run his mouth at the other crew members, criticising them for this and that. Tempers frayed. Geoff put the guy in check, but he didn't heed the warning. Just kept on shouting at the crewmen and throwing his weight around.

Another twenty-four hours passed.

With the guy issuing threats against the rest of the crew, I knew we had a serious problem on our hands. I thought it was only a matter of time before he snapped and physically attacked one of my crew. I decided to take action, and speak a few choice words to the guy about what was and wasn't acceptable on my ship.

I went down to the galley to have it out with him. It wasn't a task I looked forward to. The guy was several inches taller than me and had a wide-shouldered, heavyset frame. One punch and he'd knock my lights out.

I found him in the galley. He turned to face me head-on, and looked at me as if to say, What's yer problem?

'Now look here,' I said, my voice in check. I didn't want to inflame the scene further. Things were heated enough as they stood. 'I hire, I fire. Is that clear?'

He said nothing, so I continued.

'There's only one boss on this boat, and that's me. When you set foot aboard here, you'll do what you're told. Nae place here for people who want go around playing king. D'ye ken?'

The guy fumed, but his mouth was clamped shut. By now the rest of the crew had gathered around, watching with interest. I couldn't afford to back down, not with them looking on. I had to show them I was the boss, not this guy.

Finally, he spoke up.

'Oh, I ken all richt,' he replied. 'There's nae a decent skipper coming out a Peterhead. That's what I ken.'

He was hoping to intimidate me. But he was badly wrong.

'Ye can call me whatever you like,' I said, standing my ground and looking him dead in the eyes. 'But how about ye let me finish the trip before you decide whether I'm a guid or bad skipper? Ye cannae judge a man three days in.'

I saw anger in his eyes. Not casual anger, but burning, fiery hatred. I worried that he might swing his fists at me. Hold your ground, Jimmy, I told myself.

The guy turned briefly away from me. He searched the eyes of the other crewmen. A devilish grin swam across his lips. 'Okay then. I'm packing my bags.'

The threat was crystal clear. By stating that he intended to pack up, he thought he was hurting me and befriending the crew, standing up to the skipper. Pretending to be the big man. He made a fatal error of judgement there. The crew's opinion of the man could not have sunk any lower. By refusing to work, all he'd achieved was to double their own workload, as the guys on the deck were a man down.

'Take me home,' he said, sensing the mood had swung decisively against him. 'I'm packing up and ye'll return me to port.'

I folded my arms. 'I'll do nae such thing. If ye want to pack up, it's up to ye, but yer not gaun home till this boat's filled its boxes.'

'Fine, then.'

And with that, he brushed past me and took up a seat at the galley table, kneading his hands. That's where he stayed for three days, the duration of his trip, doing nothing except stoking the crew's resentment towards him.

It just goes to show, you can't judge a man properly till you've been with him on the North Sea. People who are perfectly pleasant ashore develop a split personality once they're floating on a body of water. I've thought a lot about why this happens, and I struggle for an explanation.

The truth of it is, the only work environments comparable to a trawler are submarines and space shuttles. You're in an extremely confined space, totally denied the luxuries of life that we all take for granted. There's no iPhones or email, and you're not free to come and go as you please. There's nowhere to hide, and a deck hand has to bed down for a hard routine of eat, work and sleep. I like to say that there's a lot of people who *can* do the job – but there's nae a lot of people who *want* to do the job. And that's the difference between good crew and bad crew: How well can you cope with being removed from society?

A funny thing happens these days when the *Amity II* sets sail. When we're ten miles clear of the coast, the mobile phone signal is lost. So before we hit the ten-mile mark, the crew will be sending their texts in a desperate frenzy, knowing that they'll be without a signal any moment, and all contact with the outside world will be cut off for the next ten days. The same happens on the reverse leg of the trip. As we close in on land, the crew will head up to the wheelhouse to check if they've got a signal. Even as we're manoeuvring through the harbour, I'll see a deck hand tending the ropes with one hand, a phone glued to his ear.

I don't notice it so much as skipper, as I have satellite phones and remote email access. But the withdrawal from society can do funny things to a man. And maybe that's why a few members of my crew have flipped.

Or perhaps it's the simpler explanation that a man begins to tire of life at sea.

Even the best skippers lose a bit of their passion for the fishing. Me included. When you're a young pup, it's like being a racehorse. At eighteen I was full of get-up-and-go, and being at sea had very little physical effect on me – apart from the seasickness. The decks on the *Responsive* and *Fidelia* used to be sectioned off with wooden boards three feet high, designed to save water and separate the fish. To shift from one side of the deck to the other, a deck hand had to hurdle these boards, hundreds of times if you were at sea for a good length of time. Us young lads would clear them at a run, breezing past the old salts who took two or three attempts to hobble over them with their sore joints and aching bones.

'Jus' ye wait til yer fifty,' the older guys said, nudging me. 'Ye won't love the sea so much then.'

What a lot of rot, I thought at the time.

Well, now I'm that age and I can see what they meant. The sea's exacted a heavy toll on my body, to the point where my passion for fishing has dimmed. I don't look ahead to trips with the same energy and enthusiasm I had when I was thirty years old. Perhaps that's also because the industry isn't as vibrant today. But when I step off the *Amity II* at the quay, my muscles are weary and my legs are stiff, and I'm thinking, If I'm being honest, being a fisherman is a job for a young man. It's not a job for those of us with a few more years under our belts.

10

THE TEAM

With all the risks and difficulties befalling a life at sea, it's important to have a crew that works well together, and who have got each other's backs. Sometimes the guy in the next bunk is the one who saves your life. When I first started fishing, it was the norm for the crew to sleep with all their clothes on: jeans, socks, shoes, sweater. I don't know why. I, for one, never bothered to follow this tradition. I've always preferred to take my breeks off before taking to my bed in my underwear.

One night aboard the *Amity II*, we were all enjoying a few hours of much-needed kip, when the watchman rushed down to the galley shouting, 'Fire!'

That single word is the worst thing you can hear on a boat. Imagine being in a building that catches fire, when you cannot escape and there's no fire service to come to your rescue. It's just you and an extinguisher. Fail to put out the flames and you're toast.

Upon hearing the alarm, I immediately sprang out of bed and made for the working deck below the galley dressed in just my undergarments. A generator we'd installed on the deck was coughing up gunmetal smoke. Flames coming out, crawling up the wall and spreading to the roof, spurred on by the air fanning in through the open doors. I could see the fire edging towards us, chewing up my boat bit by bit. I needed to act, and quick. Grabbing the fire extinguisher, I pointed the hose at the generator and sprayed foam over the flames even as it continued to run. But the smoke was beating me. It billowed down from the roof in thick, suffocating knots. My eyes watered, my throat ached, like I was swallowing glass.

I blinked and rubbed the tears out of my eyes. When I opened them again, my entire view was obscured by this black cloud. I couldn't see my exit through the smoke.

The fire overwhelmed me. I was down on my hands and knees, using a small gap between the floor and the smoke to try and fix an eye on my escape route. I breathed in the air as the smoke came down like a fog. By now the fire had engulfed almost the entire roof. The guts of the *Amity II* are lined with a marine ply that acted as fuel; in a matter of seconds I was going to be engulfed by the smoke, unable to get out. I desperately kept hosing down the generator. Not my boat, I thought. Not this time. But although I was winning the war with the fire, I feared I was going to lose the battle for my life.

Almost out of time.

Nae way out.

I saw a figure cutting a swathe through the smoke. From a distance he looked and sounded like Darth Vader. I blinked and got a closer look at the figure. Recognised the face behind the mask. Geoff, kitted out in breathing apparatus. He'd had the sense and foresight to understand what was going to happen, and had fetched the breathing apparatus we stored up in the wheelhouse. He took over control of the extinguisher and I made my exit. From there I slammed the doors and closed the air vents to stop the air from entering and fuelling the flames. Geoff quickly had the fire under control.

The whole drama lasted two or three minutes, but had threatened to annihilate my boat – and me and my crew with it. There was nowhere for us to run. If we hadn't stopped the fire, that boat would have suffered severe internal damage. The watchman who'd raised the alarm was in charge of the fish-room and he'd come down to switch off the ice machine which was when he spotted the fire. When he went to alert me and the crew, the fire was just a couple of measly flames on top of the generator. In less than a minute, it had spread its devastation across the working deck.

That day, I realised how quickly I could lose my ship.

That's all part of the risk a skipper takes each time he leaves the breakwaters and heads out to sea. It's the same with storms.

I've spoken before about how my experience on the *Fidelia* unnerved me and taught me to appreciate the sea, but I also believe that each man has his own comfort zone, conditions he's happy to trawl in and those he thinks are just too desperately bad. Some skippers are willing to push themselves to the edge. I'm not like that, though I don't avoid risk completely either. In fact, I like to think I'm in the middle somewhere. I'll accept a moderate amount of risk, but I won't put the lives of myself and my crew in reckless danger. There are colleagues of mine who have taken the risk and it's not paid off.

It comes down to faith. You've got to believe in your boat, that it'll stand up to whatever the sea will throw at it. The best skippers know their ships inside out; they feel secure when the ship's being pounded by big waves. It's a bit like a wife. You grow into a boat and gain an understanding of how she'll react in certain situations, and if there's something amiss, you will feel the change. I see a wave beating its way towards the *Amity II* today, I can predict exactly what she's going to do when that lump of water strikes. How much she'll move, and whether she'll get a wee bit of a knock.

Faith in your boat – and faith in your crew.

A skipper can have the most advanced boat in the fleet. He can use the latest technology and have the widest experience of the fishing grounds. The mannie can have all of this, but none of it will do him a jot of good, unless he can call upon a good crew.

Kevin O'Donnell joined my crew in 2004. He struck me as

a straight-talking, positive guy and as crew came and went, it became apparent that, with me and Geoff job-sharing, we were in need of someone to take the lead on the deck. Kevin came across as a happy-go-lucky kind of guy, but beneath that image was a fella who could take charge of a situation and motivate the crew to do a job. He also had that most invaluable leadership skill: he wasn't scared of having a go and trying something new.

When Kevin joined my crew, I had a tougher time figuring out what he was saying than he did with my Doric lingo, on account of his strong Irish brogue. There were an awful lot of times when he couldn't understand me and I couldn't understand him. I used to think that Kevin was a terrible bad speaker, but after several years together, I found it easier to figure out what he was telling me. Like all things aboard a boat, you adapt and change to fit the needs of others. Nowadays I find that my crew, which has included Latvians and Filipinos, are able to understand my accent. Indeed, a couple of the Latvians have even started speaking a bit of the Doric.

'Fit like te'day?' I'll say to them, asking them how they're doing.

'Nae bad,' they reply in a Russian accent.

If I'm being truthful, Kevin probably got away with murder aboard the *Amity II*. That's the kind of guy he was. But he had a special way of keeping the guys going when spirits threatened to get low, or the crew was feeling tired and longing to get home. And he wasn't shy of work. Kevin was a go-ahead kind of guy: if we had a problem, or a chore called for brute muscle, he was the first man in there, not afraid to get stuck in.

Not long after we first met, I asked Kevin, 'How on earth did ye finish up in Peterhead?'

'Me and a mate agreed to try our luck elsewhere in the world,' Kevin replied. 'We had a deal. When we got to the airport at Dublin, we'd fly to the first destination that came up on the screen. Jimmy, we were prepared to go anywhere in the world with our Irish fishing skills. Spain, Brazil, Australia. I was ready for a trip around the world.

'So we arrived at the airport. First flight we saw on the screen was . . . Glasgow.'

Having finished up at Glasgow, Kevin and his mate thought, Well, we're fishermen and we're in Scotland for the long haul now. We may as well trek up to Peterhead and find some work. That's how he happened to be on my boat. Kevin would spend several years aboard the *Amity II*. I learned a great deal about the lad during the time we worked, and lived, together. He slept two feet from me, in the bunk above my head. I like to say that Kevin slept as close to me as I do to my wife, although he wasn't in the same bed as me.

Every night he went to bed, Kevin prayed. I think that's remarkable, that a guy could find the energy and commitment to do that after a hard day's slogging. But that was the nature of Kevin. The two of us got on really well, partly, I think, because we had a similar upbringing. He was one of several kids and had to fight for his survival as a young boy. Nothing was handed to him on a plate; his family, like mine, had little money. Kevin was prepared to go to the ends of the world to make a better life for himself. He epitomised what it means to be a fisherman: the ability to rough it. It's not the kind of job where you can rise out of bed at eight-thirty in the morning, have a shower and a shave and a bowl of cornflakes while reading the newspaper before strolling down to the office and grabbing a coffee break an hour later. Work comes first. Everything else comes second.

That makes all crewmen unusual, but Kevin really shone through. For one thing, he was the only guy who dared to answer me back, and I actually respected him for that. The man spoke his mind. He was a strong-willed guy and wasn't afraid to tell me what he thought of certain decisions. We had a few conflicts down the years, but he also conceded that the skipper's word was final. If he spoke back and I said, 'Right, this is what we're gaun do,' he'd pick himself up and get on with it. No questions asked, no moaning.

Some guys treat the boat like a second family. It's somewhere familiar, where they know the faces and the routine, and there's a degree of loyalty. I like continuity in a crew. It breeds trust and friendship and it makes the long trips easier. Other guys like to jump from ship to ship. One guy on my boat was known as the joker in the pack. He was a great guy, but he went round the fleet not once, but twice. He'd come aboard the boat, stick about for a few months until we hit a bad spell.

And then on to the next port of call. Fair enough. Some guys don't like to have a steady berth. They tire quickly and want to move on to new opportunities. That's not to say they're not good hands – sometimes they are – but you don't really build up a true bond with them, in the same way that I did, for example, with Kevin.

I always regard that bond as an important part of making sure that the guys are pulling in the same direction. It doesn't have to be all sweetness and roses, of course. But having guys who actually like each other, and might easily share a pint back ashore, makes the tough days at sea tolerable. I find that with a crew that gets on well, each member will go that extra yard for his crewmates – vitally important when the guys are exhausted at the end of an eighteen-hour shift and everybody has to muck in to get the last prawns graded or shoot the gear.

Irene might have plucked the name *Amity* from the page of a dictionary, but I like to think that 'friendship' sums up the kind of man I am, or aspire to be. I don't see myself as high and mighty, lording it over the crew. My parents brought me up to believe that you always treat others how you want to be treated yourself. I've gone through life with that attitude and it hasn't done me any harm. Working my way up from that tough half-share to skipper taught me some important lessons in how to lead a crew. I'd never ask anyone to do something I wouldn't do myself. So it is that on *Amity II*, I have to take my turn to clean the toilet, same as everybody else.

If the crew see you, the *capitano*, working alongside them

and establishing a good rapport from time to time, then you'll earn their respect. The distant, aloof skipper does himself no favours by sitting up in his wheelhouse as if it's some grand castle. The skipper cannot be one of the lads, but it doesn't hurt to sometimes show you're willing to muck in.

The flipside of that is that I don't tolerate people with attitude problems as I described earlier. Someone joins my vessel with a rank attitude, then I'm sorry, but there's no room for slackers and grumblers. It comes down to this: you need to be running a happy ship, because you're out there for eight days, sometimes longer. I liken it to putting six guys in a static caravan and telling them, 'This is where you're going to work, eat and sleep, and not just for the next eight days, but for the next month, the next year and the next six years. This is it, lads.'

The real test for a crew's attitude comes when you are at sea and find yourself in the throes of a bad storm. Nothing takes more out of a man.

We'll be trawling in bad weather, thirty knots and more, chewing our fingernails as we wait for the next trawl to come back on board. Eating breakfast in such miserable conditions can get a man down. It's highly dangerous to cook while the ship lurches back and forth like a rocking horse. Everything takes more effort when you're at sea. Aye, you get used to the motion of the boat, but the stress on your muscles is intense: whether you're moving about or standing still, your body has to work hard to balance itself.

You hope the weather front passes overnight.

Then you wake up and discover it's actually worsened, blowing in excess of forty knots. The outlook for the rest of the trip is equally grim, and your only hope of making a catch in foul storms is to steal a catch in between the heavy blusters and northerly gales. You can't avoid feeling helpless; if the weather's not good for fishing, there's little you can do.

Finally, the weather takes a turn for the better. Relief courses through your veins and your heart steadies as a big catch comes in, lovely juicy prawns in the cod-end. By now you're hungry and tired and cold, but the hard work has only just begun, because the catch has to be kept in the best possible condition and processed and packed into the fishroom the moment it lands on deck. If the prawns are left outside, they'll quickly spoil and the buyer will write off a hefty cut of your total catch.

There's no tea-breaks while we grade the catch. It is work, work and more work until the last prawn has been iced up and stored below deck. If the catch is a big one, we're looking at five or six hours of grading. Meanwhile the gear's been shot and trawling, and the next haul is nearly ready to be lifted up. You've got time for a rushed meal, washed down with a cup of tea, before heading back up on deck to haul in the nets and start the grading process all over again. This routine goes on as long as there's a catch to be made. It might be eighteen or nineteen hours before you get another chance to crash in your bunk for an hour or two.

Living and working in those conditions, you've got to make

it work, and the unity of the guys only happens when you're all working towards a common goal. If there are guys who are moaning Minnies, irritable with lack of sleep and negative about the tiniest details, the bad vibe soon spreads to the rest of the crew. I think the best compliment I can pay to a guy like Kevin is that he made the bad days brighter. There's no more you can ask of a crewman.

11

OPPORTUNITY OF A LIFETIME

Peterhead is a unique town. It shaped my younger years, and, to a large extent, made me the man I am today. It's a place that has thrived with the fishing industry, enjoyed the fruits of the boom years – and suffered when the fishing dipped. I've lived in Peterhead all my life, and it remains very close to my heart.

In a town where fishing has been massively important to its people for more than two hundred years, the Fishermen's Mission has played a major role, both in the past and the present.

The Mission was founded in 1881 in order to provide support to the fishermen and their families, be it financial, spiritual or physical. There are individual Mission centres in more than seventy UK fishing ports and harbours, and the busiest ports, such as Peterhead, have a dedicated superintendent. Each

Mission has showers, washing machines and a canteen where fishermen, both current and retired, can go for a cooked breakfast or lunch and a cup of tea.

I've always been supportive of the Fishermen's Mission, and it's long been a part of my life. In Peterhead the local fishermen meet up there; it's the hub of the town. Inside it looks like a busy working man's café, fishermen popping in and out, and a noticeboard where wee lads scouting for a berth can put up their name in the hope a skipper will give them a call. The Mission has a bustling feel to it. Visitors are welcome to pop in. If you do happen to find yourself in the Mission, you'll see old salts discussing the current issues of the day, and mostly disagreeing with whatever the other guy has to say. It just goes to show – the rivalry and camaraderie between men of the sea never dies out, and the Mission provides them with a way of maintaining a close connection to the goings-on at the port.

There's an unusual routine at the Peterhead Mission. We have two sittings a day: at nine-thirty to ten o'clock in the morning, the retired deck hands arrive for a good brew and a chin wag about current affairs and who's in with a good catch. Then, at around noon, the ex-skippers come in and chat among themselves, quite happy hanging out with their own kind. Everyone's aware of this strange separation of former captains and crewmen, although we make a wee drama out of it; the two groups do speak to each other and get on fine, but the fact they arrive at different times shows up that, once you're in the wheelhouse, you cannot go back to bantering with the deck hands. It's them and you, years after you've stepped down from the fleet.

To this day, the Peterhead Mission continues to be a vital resource for the community, perhaps more than we skippers tend to think. The Mission Man, as the superintendent is known, has to look after widows and widowers, organise charity events and Christmas parties, and has a wealth of responsibilities besides. If you're sick in hospital, you can be sure the Mission Man will be the first guy to pay a visit. If you find yourself in a financial rut, the Mission Man can, to a certain degree and depending on your circumstances, provide you with help.

Peterhead is also a very religious town. To my mind this goes hand-in-hand with the fishing. The West brothers pray before each meal aboard the *Fruitful Bough*, and I myself was brought up in a Close Brethren family. The Close Brethren are very religious folk with strong beliefs about working on Sundays and such. It's part and parcel of a town that has a lot of different religions. At one point I counted more than fifteen types of denomination, which, for a town the size of Peterhead, with a population of 18,000, is pretty remarkable. There's Close Brethren, breakaway Brethren, the Church of England, the Scottish Church, Baptists, Roman Catholics, Jehovah's Witnesses, and many more besides.

When I was growing up, skippers had a deep relationship with God. That's changed now. We live in a whole different world; I reckon most fishermen in today's fleet wouldn't be able to survive if they didn't fish on a Sunday. I certainly know I couldn't do the job I'm doing if I took every Sunday off to break bread and worship. That's not intended to be disrespectful to people who do rest on the Lord's Day, but simply stating that needs must. You've got to put food on the table. My parents are still passionate Close Brethren to this day, and I admire them for it. For my own part, I do fear God and He is in my life each day.

Superstition also used to be rampant among Peterhead's fishermen. I used to follow superstitions as a young lad on the *Responsive* and *Fidelia*, when I was a wee bit gullible, but these days I believe they're a lot of rot. A skipper has plenty to worry about, from the quotas through to the upkeep of his boat, without having to busy his mind with meaningless fanciful notions. There were dozens of do's and don't's on a boat: for instance, don't say the word 'salmon' while you're at sea. As we couldn't call the fish by their real name, we referred to them in Doric as 'caul irin', 'cold iron', I guess because they looked like bars of steel in the water. If an old salt caught you saying 'salmon' aboard the boat, your backside was going to get booted for sure.

Another superstition said never to carry a box of Swan matches on to the boat. Because of the picture of the swan, you see. Back then I'd not dare contemplate taking a box on board for fear of getting a real licking from the crew. And I'm led to believe the old salts didn't like to meet the minister on their way to work, while if you whistled on a boat one of the older guys would say out the corner of his mouth, 'There'll be enough wind when the next gale comes, boy.'

I didn't subscribe to these beliefs, and I don't think a lot of the other younger lads did either. The old salts were the ones who believed all that stuff. I reckon it's a generational thing; they were guys who'd struggled to make a living in the hard days before the fishing became lucrative. Like my grandfather, many of these guys had to leave town to go and build the roads at a time when the fishing had suffered a massive decline. They'd experienced a life where forces beyond their control inflicted tremendous hardships on them. Still, I reckon a skipper and his crew make their own luck at sea, Swan matchbox or no Swan matchbox.

Superstitions aside, Peterhead's not such a bad place to live. I'm not saying there's no better places. Paradise, I'm sure, is very nice. But in the grand scheme of things, we do okay by ourselves in Peterhead. I've always been very passionate about the town, and the fishing. Aside from my family, they're the twin loves of my life.

One of my strengths is the fact that I love talking. I'll stop and chat to anyone. Down at the fish market this often comes in handy. We regularly get visitors from the big supermarket chains like Marks & Spencer, Waitrose and Sainsbury's, and I think to myself, Aye, here's a good opportunity to promote my industry.

One morning in the summer of 2005 we were at the end

of our trip, unloading the last of our boxes of prawns from the *Amity II*. I happened to notice three young ladies standing pensively at one side of the quay, looking at our catch and giggling among themselves. They were well dressed and obviously knew nothing about fish; but just as transparent was their fascination with it.

I ambled on over and introduced myself. Their accents gave them away as coming from south of the border. Figuring they were visitors from one of the big supermarkets, I explained the various species of fish we'd caught and showed them around the market and quay. They seemed curious about every detail of the fishing, and I offered to give them a tour of the boat itself. Over cups of tea in the galley, one of the girls stopped me short as I elaborated one or other point about the trade.

'We're researchers from the BBC,' the girl said, 'and we've been sent up here by BBC Birmingham to look into the possibility of doing a programme about the fishing industry. How do you feel about that, and would you be interested in helping out?'

I said I'd be glad to help, although I wasn't stunned by their offer. Other films had been made about the fishing, not all of them positive, and I figured they wanted to do a half-hour slot, maybe after the local news, nothing major. But I wasn't too negative about the proposal either. I was desperate for some good publicity for the industry, and perhaps the BBC could do us a favour.

The girls went on their way, and I thought nothing more of it.

In October, I bumped into one of the girls for a second time at the pier. We happened to be landing another catch, and she came over and said hello to me. Her name was Dina Mufti.

'Well, we've gone back to our bosses, and they want us to do some more research,' she explained. 'We think that there should be some key characters in the film, that people at home can relate to, and we think that you could be one of those characters.'

'Okay, sounds good to me,' I replied. Again, I wasn't making a big song and dance out of it. As far as I was concerned, she wanted me to be in a fishing film, I was a fisherman, so it made perfect sense.

That was as much as I heard about it for several months until one morning in January 2006, when Peterhead is at its darkest and coldest. I left my fishing agent's office after attending to some business, and chanced upon Dina in the street.

'We were looking for you, as it happens,' she said. I noticed a guy standing next to her armed with a tripod and camera. 'I've got some great news. We've been given a budget to make the programme, and we're ready to go!'

I raised my hands. 'Hold on,' I replied. Although I was impressed with their enthusiasm and desire to get the ball rolling, I also had to be careful to do things properly. 'It's not as simple as jumping on the boat with me,' I continued. 'We need to get you Survival at Sea certificates, insurance . . .'

Dina nodded.

'We have a health and safety guy at the BBC. He's going to come up and look at the boat.'

That'll be a laugh, I thought. I knew from experience that health and safety officers and fishing trawlers did not go well together. Their job is to protect the wellbeing of employees. And for all the regulations and safety equipment, and the guidelines that boats are built according to these days, it's still the case that there's a million safer places to be. There is no getting away from the dangers you face when you set sail.

I suppose because I'd been the first point of contact at Peterhead harbour, the production team decided to get me heavily involved in the filming side of things, in helping them to understand what needed to be done before a film crew could go out to sea. I introduced the team to John Buchan, skipper of the *Ocean Venture*, and James West, saying that I thought they'd make ideal subjects for the documentary.

The cynicism of some of the other guys in the fleet probably had something to do with it too. Quite a few skippers were sceptical about letting cameras come in and film us as we went about our business. They were never sure what a cameraman would do with the footage once he got back ashore, and were afraid that they'd be painted in a bad light. I never saw it that way: the BBC team was open with me from the start, and I've a strong sense of when an opportunity is there to be grasped. To my eyes, bringing millions of people on to our boats could only be a good thing, in terms of drumming up attention and awareness of the difficulties we faced day in, day out.

After a week we'd completed enough training to feel more confident about getting the crew on my boat. Dina was a class act, a great lass who knew how to energise everybody. She organised things and pulled strings when they needed pulling.

The health and safety guy from the BBC made his trip up from London to assess the boat. He took a look at the living conditions and potential dangers and said, 'If you want me to sign this thing off, it's not going to happen.'

With Dina's know-how and determination to get things done, we found a way around this problem. Essentially it boiled down to the fact that the film crew had to accept they were in a high-risk area, and if they wanted to come aboard the *Amity II*, then by all means they were welcome – but they did so at their own peril. As long as they understood the consequences of their actions and the risks they were taking, I was delighted to have them along for the ride.

'How many people are you intending to take aboard?' I asked them.

'We'd like four,' came the reply.

I shook my head. 'Can't do it. There's only four or five fishermen on the boat total, and we don't have the space for a double crew. Ye can bring one guy.'

One, it turned out, wasn't enough. A film crew ashore consisted of a producer, a cameraman, a director, a gopher and a soundman: too many tasks for a single person to perform. In the end, we settled on a compromise of a two-man team. The cameraman, Matt Bennett, had to be the director, producer and general dogsbody, while his colleague Kiff McManus was on sound.

We had no script to follow, no directions were given to us. The idea was that the film crew would come aboard purely to observe and gain a better understanding of life at sea for the benefit of people at home. At first, because I didn't know who I was dealing with, I didn't permit them to leave the comfort of the wheelhouse. I had nightmarish visions of one of them getting tossed overboard in a hoolie.

As I got to know them better, I allowed them to move and film more freely around the boat. But on that first night – the opening scenes of the first episode of the documentary, with a storm brewing and my nets stuck fast on the seabed – I exercised caution. I was also very conscious of the camera in those first few days. Here I was, allowing Matt to film me as I went about my job and my life. I had no idea what the results would look like. Matt was a great guy, and it didn't take long for a good level of trust to build up between us. He wanted to make a genuine, honest documentary about fishermen, and why we do what we do.

That first stormy evening, however, I was new to Matt and the world of reality television.

'Jimmy, what are you thinking just now?' Matt asked as I tried in vain to free my gear from the seabed.

What was I thinking?

If ye don't get this camera out of my face it's gaun over the rail!

Losing a net was failure for a skipper, and the embarrass-ment of having my mistakes played out to millions of people stuck in my throat. But I learned an important lesson at that particular moment. Either I put on a front, acting nice and polite, and insincere, or lowered my guard and allowed the public to see the real, uncut life of a fisherman and his ordeals.

I took the decision to be open and speak my mind freely, with clarity and honesty. Whether the viewers agreed with what I did or said – that was up to them, not me. I just told it how I saw it. Considering the positive comments we got as a result of the show, I think we achieved a realistic depiction of what it's really like to spend more than half your life above a violent body of water, hundreds of miles from your loved ones.

As well as filming aboard the *Amity II* and a couple of other ships, including James West's *Fruitful Bough*, the production team decided they'd film in and around the community of Peterhead, integrating stories of the town into the series. I thought this was a great idea, and showed them around some of the important sites and characters. I took them to the Fishermen's Mission and the creel men down at the harbour. They got some great footage of the different sides of the fish-ing legacy in the town, but sadly, when it came to airing the series, all these on-shore scenes ended up on the cutting-room floor.

I don't blame the BBC for this – it's simply because the at-sea footage was so good that they didn't have the time or space to use the other stuff. But it still made me feel uneasy, because I'd introduced them to these various characters, and these people all assumed they were going to be on TV. That's how TV works, though: the editor decides how a particular programme will run, and his primary interest is in making a show that will excite the viewers.

The success of *Trawlermen* took me back at first. I don't know quite what I expected of the series. I thought it could be popular, but I didn't foresee quite how popular. And because I'd been so involved in the series from the very beginning, and they featured me, Kevin and the rest of the crew fairly heavily from the start, the fame of the show also rubbed off on me. Celebrity, or whatever they might call it, never concerned me: I was just excited that so many British people were taking an active interest in Peterhead's fleet.

It really only hit home how much of a difference I'd made when Libby Woodhatch, the CEO of Seafood Scotland, a government body that promotes the industry, phoned me up one day.

'Jimmy,' she said, 'do ye ken, you've done more for this industry than if we'd had a five-million-pound promotion budget on national television.'

Libby's words encouraged me at a time when some people were criticising the show, saying I should've done this or that. I merely pointed out to such people that I had no say in the editing of the series. I said what I said at sea, telling it how it was. I didn't dress it up. Some people have issues with that approach, but knowing that people like the CEO of Seafood Scotland were on my side, helped to put my mind at ease.

The magic of the *Trawlermen* series was to use the medium of TV to give people a genuine insight into life at sea – a world that they're rarely, if ever, exposed to. At the peak of its success, the series was pulling in five million viewers a night, so people responded to it in droves, that's for sure. We had guys like Chris Evans saying they were huge fans.

On a few occasions, the interest surrounding the show involved me personally. I once went on Radio Four to defend myself against a London cab driver, over the claim made in the documentary that being a trawlerman was 'Britain's most dangerous job'. Someone else reckoned that the cabbies had the most dangerous job, on account of the road rage and mental stress of driving in a built-up city. The cabbie argued his side of the coin, I argued mine. I don't know who won – both of us probably claimed victory. I said I reckoned I could drive a cab, but could he do a fisherman's job?

I hadn't expected the attention that would be placed on me, besides the fantastic publicity we secured for the fleet as a whole. I started to really notice it when Irene refused to go to the local supermarket with me, on account of the people coming up or simply looking at me as I went about my day. I suppose it was strange for the locals to see a Peterhead guy appearing on primetime TV.

People come up to me all the time now. It's not out of the ordinary for me to go down to the pier and be approached by a couple who've journeyed up from London and headed down to the harbour to get a look at the *Amity II* on the off-chance they might bump into me. They ask for a picture and want to share a few words, and to be perfectly honest, I'm happy to oblige. I've been fortunate in that I was able to cope with being in the public arena exceptionally well. It goes back to the fact I love interacting with people and can quite happily talk away for hours on end about what I do, how I do it and why. Maybe if I was on the shy side, being on the front-line of the cameras would have fazed me.

So I never had to 'learn to live' with the attention. A good job, too – because it doesn't matter where we go now, as a family; I get recognised at airports, on holiday and in restaurants. I enjoy talking to the folk I meet, but I don't let such things go to my head. My parents brought me up to understand how important it was to keep my feet on the ground and never to be big-headed. To me, getting noticed is just one of those things.

Even to this day, I'll receive emails from people intending to visit Scotland from as far afield as Australia, wanting to make sure I'm in port when they plan to visit, so they can go on a detour to Peterhead. They tell me how much they love the show; and I'm proud to have helped put Peterhead on the map. From that perspective, I guess, the town I was born and grew up in is now known not just throughout the UK, but worldwide. It's truly been a privilege to be part of the whole thing.

Another benefit from the popularity of *Trawlermen* was the ways in which I could put myself, and my newfound place in the public arena, to good use with the Fishermen's Mission. None of the skippers or crew received money from the BBC in return for the show, nor did we ask for a penny. Our desire to take part in the series wasn't motivated by cash, but by a desire to promote the industry and show people a different side than perhaps they were reading in the papers or seeing on the news. On the back of this, the Mission contacted me and said, Right, the fishing industry is getting all this publicity – can we use you to help with the Mission's cause? I was delighted and agreed there and then to do what I could.

So for a year the Mission used Jimmy Buchan as the face of the industry, and because a fair number of people recognised me as the skipper, they donated to the Mission on the back of it. Every donation was vital: the Mission is a charity and depends entirely on the nation's generosity for its continued existence and ability to support the community. I also wrote letters to individual donors, encouraging them to carry on supporting their local Mission.

The success of my initial involvement led to my invitation to join the local advisory council in Peterhead. I'd helped the Mission nationally, and now I had the privilege of playing a hands-on role locally. Being on the committee allowed me to use my expertise to assist in the running of the Peterhead Mission, where a key part of our goal was raising donations.

Each August we hosted a big open day at the port. People ran food stands and sold their wares, and the event attracted thousands of people to the harbour. We also took the decision one year to open *Amity II* to the general public, although the clamour to get a look caught me by surprise. The queues were massive; it was like people trying to get on to the set of *EastEnders* or *Coronation Street*. *Amity II*'s a small boat, and there's not space for an 'in' queue and another for people going out. We had up to twenty or even thirty people on the boat at any one time, plus myself and a few helpers, but thousands of people were desperate to come on board including, dare I say it, elderly citizens. I worried they'd have a problem going down staircases that in reality are more like sheer drops, but happily we managed to get on board most of the people who wanted to come. At five o'clock, after several hours of tours guided by yours truly, the superintendent finally had to cut off the queue and call it a day. Still, the excitement *Amity II* created that day was phenomenal, and it inspired many people to donate to the Mission.

The following year, myself and a colleague by the name of Arthur McDonald decided to do something a bit different. Arthur runs a fish processor called Select Shellfish; he buys and processes on my behalf some of the prawns I catch. We set up a stall between us to cook langoustines for the locals. The idea was inspired. Lots of British people have only ever tasted shrimps, not prawns, as is borne out by the fact that, of the many tons of shellfish Arthur processes at his plant each day, only a tiny percentage is destined for the domestic market. Giant lorry loads head for the Continent, while a paltry pallet is shipped elsewhere in the UK.

No cook is complete without his tunic and hat. I blagged a costume from a local chef, which drew a few laughs from the punters. We raised a healthy amount of money on that day. On another occasion, I was asked to go to Pembrokeshire to promote the Mission. The following year, I spoke at an international Christian convention in London (the Mission was run on Christian principles by its founder, Ebenezer Joseph Mather, and continues the tradition to this day, although all faiths are welcomed and supported equally).

Skippers contribute to the Mission, but it's an uphill task every year to meet the running costs. The Peterhead Mission has to generate more than half its funding from the local community. Everyone chips in, from the fishermen to young mothers opening up baking stalls at fetes.

Whenever the Mission asks me to do something, the answer's yes. I come from the coal-face of the industry and if they feel that it heightens people's awareness of the Mission, then great. I'm also conscious of the fact that I won't be in the frontline of the public eye for ever. Everyone gets their fifteen minutes of fame: this is mine, and I intend to use it for good purposes. And I believe in the purpose of the Mission. The superintendents work awfully hard. When a man's lost at sea, it's the job of the superintendent to deliver the terrible news to the family. Modern communications have changed the way that's done, but in former times he'd knock on the door of the household concerned, the woman would answer, and he'd place his cap in his hand.

'Yer husband is at sea; the vessel is presumed lost, with nae trace of ship or crew.'

Us skippers talk about how tough life is for us. Well, there cannot be many harder jobs than having to inform a family that their father, husband, brother or son has been claimed by the sea. And his job didn't end there. He'd comfort the grief-stricken family, supporting them in whatever way he could, for years to come if need be.

I remember reading about a study which stated that for every 100,000 fishermen, 103 die at work. Fifty times more than any other profession. Alongside the horror stories, tragedies and near misses every fisherman's experienced, those numbers lay bare the risk of the trawling. When we go out to sea, some of us don't come back.

Despite that knowledge, the reality of losing a man still hits you to your core.

In April 2009, Kevin West, skipper of the *Ryanwood*, fell overboard. He'd been on a routine trip when, one breezy afternoon, his crew realised they hadn't seen him on board for an hour. After a search of the boat came up empty-handed, they began to fear the worst – that Kevin had gone over the rails. The crew frantically retraced their route, hoping to locate him, but to no avail. Search and rescue teams were called in to help with the hunt, along with an RAF helicopter and an RNLI lifeboat. Seventeen other boats also joined in the rescue operation once the crew on the *Ryanwood* put out the Mayday distress signal.

It's unusual for a skipper to be lost, rather than a crewman, because he's usually tucked away in the wheelhouse where there's no danger of going overboard. No one knows how Kevin West came to his end; it was as if he simply vanished off the face of the earth.

Kevin's death was a huge shock to the entire industry. I knew him personally; he was a genuinely nice lad and a good skipper. He worked through the same fish-selling office as me and I'd see him each time I was in port. We'd discuss the issues of the day regarding the fishing, and I found him to be a very vocal, active guy in Peterhead. Suddenly you go down to the pier one day and the thought hits you like a fist: *I'll never see Kevin again*. It's very hard to come to terms with, and it rams home to you how precious life is. It can be there one minute, and gone the next. Don't let it pass you by.

The previous August, Charles Bruce, the youngest skipper in the fleet, in charge of the *New Dawn*, lost a man at sea off the coast of Wick. He was an agency worker from the Philippines by the name of Ronaldo Benitez. Charles dived into the water to try and rescue Benitez, but the sea was too fierce and his crew had to lift him to safety. Charles ended up suffering from hypothermia.

Skipper, deck hand, agency worker: we in the fleet all feel equally the death of someone in the fishing. When a man's lost at sea, your first thought is, That's someone's son, and perhaps someone's dad or husband too. I've become accustomed to many things on the North Sea: the gales and hoolies, the cold and the dark, the loneliness. But one thing I will never, ever grow used to is death. Whenever the sea claims a man's life, it sends a jolt up my spine.

There's a local Doric saying we have: 'Ill is easy gotten.' You have to learn to love life, and value and cherish it, because you don't know who will lose their life next, or when. The BBC came looking for drama when they turfed up in Peterhead with their cameras and sound mikes and producers, but they weren't expecting two good men to die. What it did – to us, to them, to the entire community – was to serve a tragic, poignant reminder that we can make boats safer, improve communications and radar technology, but we cannot guarantee a man's safety. Fishing has, and will probably remain, a career that is marked by death and loss.

When I look back over my long career in the fishing, I realise how very lucky I've been. All the storms that came at me – if the *Amity* had lain flat on its beam ends and never returned upright, or the freak wave on the *Fidelia* had swept me overboard, I might not have made it home alive. I know of at least seven Peterhead vessels lost at sea with all hands. And just in case a fisherman forgets those terrible incidents, the North Sea throws up its own grim reminders: the wrecks of these fishing vessels have been located and charted in my fishing plotters, and we sometimes find ourselves navigating around them during our trips at sea. At such moments, I make sure I pay my respects. You never know when it's your time.

12

A LINE IN THE SAND

Times have changed, in more ways than one. The industry of today is a very different place from thirty years ago, and each day presents fresh challenges and obstacles for the fleet to overcome.

The North Sea plays host to a huge variety of fisheries, and that's down to the fact that there's an incredibly rich environment lurking beneath the waves. I often think it must be like rush hour in a big city down there. But the existence of a diverse underwater world a few miles from our coastline hasn't had much impact on our eating habits.

In the UK, the langoustine market is non-existent – other than scampi, which is the tail end of the prawn, cut off, breaded and sold in pubs. Apart from that, your average punter in Britain isn't interested in prawns. I think that we, as a people, don't enjoy seafood as an eating experience. We stick to the tried-and-tested battered fish and chips, and other than that, seafood hardly comes into our diet. There's plenty of rich dishes in the UK, from Chinese to Indian, Mexican to French, but it seems that there's nae space for the fishes. It's the same story with monkfish. Megrim too, a less popular fish that is up to sixty centimetres long, a type of flatfish with a bigger head. These are fishes that introduced me to global markets, yet there's little market for them in the UK.

Most of my sale is made in Spain and France, with a little going to Italy. During the making of the *Trawlermen* series, we managed to follow a catch of prawns all the way from the fish market at Peterhead to its final destination, a restaurant in Belgium. I'm not sure they were my catch, but they were definitely Scottish prawns. To be able to sit in a Michelin-starred restaurant in a leafy suburb in Brussels, eating your own product cooked in all its glory, got me thinking that the Europeans really know how to create a genuine seafood experience. Sitting there, I felt honoured to be representing my colleagues in the Peterhead fleet. It gave me great pleasure, as a catcher of langoustine, to know that we are producers to the world. Without fishermen like myself, taking great risks every time we sail out of port, nobody would have the opportunity to eat langoustine.

We've been here before, as fishermen, and we'll no doubt be here again in years to come. We've certainly had to face up to some terrible hardships and blows over the years. But none have been more bitter, and avoidable, than the decommissioning schemes.

The decommissioning schemes were, in my opinion, badly misguided in terms of their execution. More than that. They were a farce; the worst example of the government trying to do something on the cheap, and good, honest people paying the price for it. The idea behind the schemes was to reduce capacity so that the vessels left in the fleet could flourish. The idea was logical, if painful. But the way the government went about the task was wrong. In fact, they allowed the vessel to come out of the water, but the retiring skipper got to keep his quota. By letting the skippers retain their quotas, the guys who stayed at sea had no more quota to fish for. This created a bizarre situation called the 'Slipper Skipper' – fishermen who don't fish, but lease out their quotas to the active skippers in the fleet. Some guys get huge financial rewards from their quota, and they don't even have a boat.

I had to get a bank loan to secure my fish quota. The only way I could make my vessel legal was to go out, borrow money, and then purchase fish from a slipper skipper. It was insane, and it left a bad taste in my mouth, but I had no choice. If I didn't up my quota and get into that rat race, I'd be an also-ran, a has-been.

For the first few years after the second decommissioning scheme in 2005, though, life was really good. Prices stabilised, and for the first time in the longest time, the industry felt that it had a bright future. In 2006 I decided that, with the fishing trade in a healthy state and the future looking bright, it'd benefit me to have a rotating crew.

Ever since the 1970s, when oil was discovered a hundred miles off the coast of Peterhead, fishing has found itself in direct competition with the oil for manpower. If you arrive at Aberdeen airport, the first thing you'll notice is the posters everywhere advertising rigging companies and equipment. To the south of Peterhead, at Cruden Bay, North Sea oil is brought ashore, while north, at St Fergus, gas is landed. The fishing's literally stuck in the middle, feeling the pressure from both sides.

The oil rigs have drained the fleet of talent. I've no axe to grind with the oil companies: it's a free world and they can set whatever wages and shifts that work for them. It took an awful lot of good guys out of the fishing, though. It's a sorry state of affairs when a fleet goes through two massive decommissioning schemes, loses more than half its vessels, and yet the surviving boats still cannot get a full crew to go out fishing. We should've had the opposite, men queuing up for a berth.

I had a balanced crew with experienced and hard-working men like Geoff Phillips and Kevin O'Donnell. At the same time I understood that oil rigs are sometimes a more attractive prospect for a man, because of the amount of free time he gets between shifts. I've got to match this, I thought. So I dreamt up the idea of paying a crew to remain in port; that way they'd have more time off, because as one crew prepared to head out to sea the other was returning to land.

I was willing to do that because I wanted to go to sea with men that I trusted and could depend on – guys I had respect for. By that time Kevin had been with me for several years and he wasn't just a member of my crew, he was a friend. I imagine most of his friends were working on the oil rigs, having three weeks off to play golf while Kevin had to slog his guts out on the *Amity II*. A man's head gets turned when he sees these things, and I cannae blame him.

I've no doubt that good young trawlermen are quitting the industry because the wages no longer make sense to them. I'd be the first to give my crew a pay rise if I could afford it, but diesel costs me up to £1,000 a day whereas ten years ago it cost me £250 per day. It's simply not possible to give the crew more money if fish prices aren't going up to offset the dramatic increase in diesel cost, with the result that guys can be at sea for ten days and be earning less than the national average.

Financial aid would help reduce the strain on everyone, but where would the aid come from? The farmers get aid from the government, and I know that the French slapped a two per cent tax on fish and shellfish coming in from Britain in order to subsidise the diesel costs for their skippers.

At least the crewmen have the choice of leaving to find alternative work. The skippers are lumbered with huge bank loans. They can't just up sticks and quit.

Around this time, my dear friend Sandy Watt took the painful decision to sell his beloved boat, the *Fruitful Harvest*. He'd spent more than twenty-five years seine-net trawling, and although his vessel was a wooden boat from an older generation, it had served him well. He ran a tight ship, a happy crew. All in all, Sandy was a top-class skipper.

His decision didn't shock me; the truth is, I'd seen it coming for a while. He called me up one day, about six weeks prior to his decision, and instantly I understood that the old spark which I'd always associated with Sandy had vanished. He was normally such an optimistic guy when it came to the fishing: positive about the industry, positive about his part in it. Almost overnight, something had changed. He no longer had the heart to continue.

Before my next trip out, I said to Irene, 'Do ye ken, I've a funny feeling Sandy's gaun leave the industry.'

The very next week, he did it. He called me up by telex. We made contact on the radio.

'That's it,' he said simply, his voice flat and dull. 'I'm finished.'

I landed a few days later and made it my urgent business to go and speak to him about his decision. It's not like retiring from a job; a skipper's boat is his way of life, it's an extension of himself. Deciding to hang up his oilskins is the toughest decision any man can make.

Sandy was pretty upset about selling on the *Fruitful Harvest*, but it was also clear to me that he'd made up his mind and there'd be no going back. Leaving the North Sea was, I knew, a big ordeal for him emotionally, but it's one that every skipper has to come to terms with eventually, including myself.

Nowadays Sandy has a job working in the control room for the port authority. I'm glad he's moved on and found something to do that keeps him connected to the fishing.

In 2007, the industry took a turn for the worse, and we found ourselves on the brink of disaster.

Just as in the 1970s and '80s the whitefish gold rush had created an explosion in boat-building, now there was a drive to build, and convert, boats to harvest langoustines. Ten years ago, I gambled on the prawns and suddenly everyone else had the same idea. I couldn't blame them. Whitefish quotas were impossible to acquire and the days a quota permitted a skipper to catch were being cut, whereas the quotas in the prawn fishery were plentiful and the days were generous to boot.

The rush of boats to prawns saturated the market. Happening as it did at the start of the recession, this generated a perfect storm. Not only did we have an over-supply of prawns, forcing the prices down, but when the recession proper kicked in, the processors had to realign the price they were prepared to pay for the langoustines in order to stay in business.

As a businessman, I was prepared to absorb a couple of bad years. I reasoned that we'd had some very good years, and one or two slightly worse ones wouldn't damage my business beyond repair. But our industry's problems didn't happen in isolation. We had a double squeeze: the recession, and legislation.

We went into the following year knowing that there'd be a non-negotiable ten per cent cut in the amount of fish we were permitted to catch. At the same time, fuel prices went through the roof. Faced with those terms, a fisherman starts to think to himself, 'Well, I'm not gaun make a profit this year, or even the next owing to that cut.' He feels the noose tightening. He has no room for manoeuvre. Higher fuel prices. Lower fish numbers, while fish prices are dropping so steeply you'd mistake it for a cliff-face. Banks calling in their loans. My margins were squeezed to the point where some weeks I was running my boat to the favour of the crew instead of my business.

As a skipper in charge of paying my guys on a share basis, I used to deduct my running costs from the gross and split the rest down the middle between the vessel and the crew, fifty-fifty. I was aware that if, after the increased running costs and lower prices, I gave the crew only fifty per cent in return for the work they did, none of them would stick around for very long. In order to keep my business going – because I needed a crew to earn money – I decided to make sure the crew still got a reasonable pay. I had little choice but to take it out of the vessel's share.

But in such a deflated market, the boat's income simply wasn't able to meet the needs of the crew. With the recession, and faced with competition from the oil industry, it became a struggle to hold on to Kevin and other steady, dependable crewmen.

Paying guys to sit around Peterhead eventually proved

unsustainable. The problem is, once you've created a precedent, people don't want to change back to the way things were. I'd introduced a system that was better than the share model traditionally used on boats and guys like Kevin were reluctant to return to being paid on a share basis. It's not hard to understand their feelings: how many employees at any company, up and down the land, would voluntarily accept a twenty or thirty per cent cut in their salary? Given the job they did, I held nothing against Kevin for looking at other ways of earning a living. He's a keen guy who wants to get on in life, and he could see that the fishing industry was entering a slump.

One day, he might come back to the fishing. Who knows? Usually, however, when these guys go on to another world, they start to realise that there's life beyond fishing, and their desire to return quickly evaporates. I'm led to believe that Kevin now works on a barge for an oil company out in Egypt. He probably has a more regular schedule, and the comfort of a steady, secure income. I can't begrudge the man that – he made the right decision given his circumstances. One thing's for sure though; he's been sorely missed aboard my boat.

In the last few years, maintaining a crew has been a tremendous challenge. It's painful when guys leave, because you've struck up a good bond with them, and it also wounds my professional pride. If you've got a big turnover of crew, then you're failing as a skipper. The only consolation I had – if you can even call it such a thing – is that I didn't let my crew down because of any action I took as the skipper.

Back when I skippered the original *Amity* there were hundreds of vessels in the fleet and every vessel had a young lad. Sometimes two. It made for a good mix in the crew, and created a chain of experience: the married men who passed their experience and skills on to the younger, single lads, teaching them the ins and outs of being a successful deck hand. That picture's changed.

We cannot get young people into the fishing any more. Sure, we have agency crews. I've employed guys from Latvia and across the world, and they do a good job; in fact, if it hadn't been for the influx of agency workers from Eastern Europe and the Philippines, I think that the industry might have collapsed in Peterhead in 2008. But they won't be the Peterhead skippers of the future. They stay for a year, then return home.

When I was a teenager, you had to fight your way to a berth on a boat. People wanted to be first mates and skippers: that was the dream. Now, if I place an advert in the local paper, asking if some young guy wants to come to sea next week, I'll be lucky to get a phone call.

Fishing isn't seen as an attractive trade these days. Part of that is money. But maybe it's also partly down to young lads being afraid to graft a wee bit. I understand that farmers have the same problem, with a good number of fruit pickers coming from Eastern Europe because the local kids don't want to get their hands dirty. Of course, we can get machinery to make life easier; nets that last longer, TVs and Sky Plus and email access at sea. But it's still hard work. Everything else in this world gets easier. Not the fishing, because the one thing you cannot change is the weather and the fact a man has to be prepared to spend an awful lot of his time away from home in a hostile environment.

Young crews have completely changed; in my day, I wouldn't have dared not turn up to go on a fishing trip. That was considered a cardinal sin. If word got around the fleet, 'Jimmy Buchan dinnae turn up fir work,' you'd have been black-marked as someone unreliable, making it impossible to secure a berth on another ship. But young people nowadays seem to think it's cool not to show. They don't seem to appreciate that it's not me they're letting down, but their crew-mates, because it's those guys who will ultimately suffer – the four remaining crewmen have to pick up the slack and do the job of the absent fifth.

Whenever I get a young lad coming aboard the *Amity II*, I'm sure to tell him, 'If you're nae gaun to come in, do the honourable thing and ring me and tell me. Dinnae hae me thinking yer turning up if ye don't intend to.'

Invariably, he nods.

Then, of course, it rolls around to two o'clock on a Saturday afternoon and I'm still waiting for the lad to arrive. I bumped into one lad a few weeks after he'd neglected to tell me he wasn't up for the fishing. Met him at the local supermarket.

'Uh, I never got yer text,' he said, reaching for a quick excuse.

Absolute rot. I know he received my text – this was a guy whose mobile phone was never more than six inches away from his ear. His track record preceded him; I was later told that he did the same on a previous boat.

For every slacker, however, you do find diamonds in the rough. I've got two young guys on the *Amity II* now, both with aspirations to be skippers, and committed to making the most out of the opportunities in front of them, in what is a very challenging industry. Guys like that give me great joy, because there's nothing I want more than to see promising fishermen achieve success and support them to that end; and it's great for the town too, to keep the fire burning in what is a large and significant part of our heritage.

And it's a heritage we have to fight hard to keep, battling against bureaucrats who want to blame the fishermen for everything that happens to the seas. To give one example: for twenty-six years, without fail, I've taken a vessel out of port, and perhaps ninety-eight per cent of my voyages have been a success. Only on a couple of occasions have I actually had to give up and return home. In all that time, I have never once seen a fishery vessel taking data of where I fish.

That's why I can't understand the scientists and their claims about the fishing industry. Where are they getting their information from? I'm guessing they go to an area I've trawled in once I'm done with it, take their analysis in the middle of the day and report back that there's nothing in that spot.

My argument is, you could tow that self-same patch of sea in the dark and find it brimming with life. Understanding the sea is all about experience and knowledge. That's why the best scientists are the skippers. We've worked these grounds for generations, and no degree or doctorate can buy the local knowledge of the Peterhead fleet. We know that the fish are busiest at daybreak and the gloaming, and that the grounds vary in activity.

If you don't work a fishing ground, it can become fallow and lifeless. This is something that I experienced back when I was still a fairly young, rookie skipper. We followed this mannie on a beam trawler as he was going up and down. A beam trawler is a very simple bottom-trawling vessel with a metal beam holding open the mouth of the net. It's used for hunting prawns and flatfish. He was going down to a spot the day before us and getting a good haul of plaice. The next day I'd make a good catch of haddock in the exact same spot. What I reckon he was doing was disturbing the seabed, sending up different crustaceans, and creating a feed for the haddock. In fact this guy helped my business – although he didn't realise it at the time!

It's not easy to be a trailblazing fisherman today. Government legislation no longer allows a skipper to be innovative. He's constrained by the laws on bycatch – fish he's caught that isn't his main quota species – and the one-net rule that stipulates he can only have one type of fishing gear on board his vessel. On the *Amity* we'd carry whitefish trawls and nephrop trawls, which allowed us to be flexible and experiment on new bits of fishing ground. Those rules have single-handedly killed off skippers who wanted to try new things. They stifle a skipper's freedom. I honestly feel that's creating a recipe for disaster: because if the next young generation of skippers cannot afford to innovate, then how on earth are we supposed to find and catch species as the food chain of the North Sea evolves?

The alternative is, we let the fishery in Peterhead die a slow death.

The port is a symbol of what's happened to the Blue Toon. It was always the focal point of activity in Peterhead. It still is – the total value of catch landed in Peterhead port in 2008 was £117 million, so the fishing continues to play a major role. But today you can go for a gentle stroll down the quay and maybe see two or three boats in dock. Thirty years ago, you'd have been lucky to walk along without being blown over by a fork-lift.

There was a bit of humour and joviality in the air in those days. The banter flowed and the larking about put a smile on everyone's face. It was a bustling place to be, and you had the impression that the port was going places.

Now skippers across the fleet live with incredible pressure. In the old days, skippers recently returned to port would stand on the quay, laughing and swapping tales, engaging in a bit of banter and sipping a hot cup of tea. When I go down to the quay today, I see skippers with hunched shoulders, their faces worn with despair. And I look at these poor guys and think to myself, Who's looking out for their interests? Who's putting the fishermen first? They're all self-employed, they have no pensions or company salaries to protect them. Instead, they're battered about by the powers-that-be, treated with less dignity than the fish they catch.

I fish. That's what I do. Today, however, I feel more like a criminal, persecuted by distant powers, simply for doing the job I love. My quota dictates that I can catch a certain amount of prawns, and that bycatch – haddock and cod – can only make up a small fraction of my total catch. In practice, I have to dump such fish overboard in order to guarantee I don't return an excess of bycatch to port. A valuable resource, which God put on this earth, has to be dumped back in the water for no reason other than someone sitting behind a desk and deciding that's what's best for the skippers.

We're heading down a path where the pressure on our shoulders will be too great to bear, and the industry collapses. Every year, the days we're allowed to fish at sea, and the quota numbers themselves, are cut and cut. They're cutting to the bone, and there will come a point when they realise they've chopped all the way through, and there's nothing left.

The more fish that we have to return to sea because of lack of quota, the longer we have to remain at sea in order to bag marketable catch to return to port. It's a vicious circle, and soon we might find ourselves in a situation where waste is outlawed altogether. Are we then going to unwittingly change the marine environment again?

I say 'again', because, in my mind, we've already changed the environment. The North Sea is a complicated ecosystem and the balance shifts over time. Today I still fish in areas that I used to work in as a young lad, twenty-five or thirty years ago, when we were catching predominantly cod and haddock. But there's a difference now. In those same areas, I'm catching very little cod and haddock but lots and lots of prawns. The cod definitely have become scarcer in those areas. The question is, Why? I don't think we overfished them. Instead, the cod moved. What's happened is that the weather today is milder; the cod has moved north in search of colder water, and with less whitefish and a degree or two change in the temperature of the sea, the prawns have been able to flourish. And there's another possibility: Have the prawns come on due to us disturbing the seabed with returned catch and interfering with the feeding chain?

If the North Sea cools again and the cod ever come back, then it's likely that the prawn stocks in the North Sea will decrease. And if the cod do come back, and they eat the prawns and cause the prawn stocks to decline, will the scientists blame the fishermen, as they've been quick to do in the past?

In fact the cod *are* returning. Today, I hear my colleagues are constantly steaming away from cod. There's so many cod, we cannot get clear of them in the upper echelons of the North Sea. Cod everywhere. This isn't circumstantial evidence, it's fact. We now have closed areas of fishing ground around the

North Sea. If a trawl tow is taken in an area and there's found to be more than forty cod, of all sizes, in that forty-minute tow, that means there's hundreds of cod in that twenty-square-mile area, and it has to be closed off to commercial fisheries for a three-week period. In the first nine months of 2008, we had more than a hundred closed-off areas in the North Sea.

If we had a shortage of cod, we'd have no closed-off areas. It looks to me like they've shot themselves in the foot with that one.

At the same time, when it comes to the fish species we *are* allowed to catch the industry is hampered by ever more limiting quotas. The shellfish is an excellent example. In 2009, prawns were the highest earners for the Scottish fishing fleet. Shellfish fishermen such as myself are significant contributors to the Scots economy; we create a demand for engineers, net makers, accountants and deck hands. When people talk about local economies, they mean guys like me. Yet shellfish quotas are being decreased year-on-year.

The next most profitable industry is the herring and mackerel of the enormous pelagic ships. Yet they operate in a very select market and cost millions of pounds to construct. In fact, there's only about twenty pelagics in the entire fleet, because one vessel does the work of twenty older boats. The pelagics do what they do very well; but it's the small businesses from the trawlermen which represent the lifeblood of our communities, and they're the ones who stand to lose out when it comes to each new wave of regulations.

I'm a prawn skipper. That's what I do, and I love doing it. I can't escape the fact, though, that I was partly pushed into that market by the EU restricting our freedom of movement. The lack of opportunities in the whitefish meant I had to divert into another fishery before I was driven out of business.

The EU's response to this is, 'We're trying to restore stock levels for the future.'

And I'd say, '*What* future?'

A combination of bad government policy and EU legislation has choked us to the point of cutting off our blood supply. Go on as we are now and there will be no more boats left to fish once my generation retires.

If the government truly believed the scientists, then they should embark on a third decommissioning scheme, and let everyone get out with their dignity intact. They should say, 'Okay, we will have this many ships in the fleet, and not one more nor one less. This will give you all a sustainable stock.' That way, no one's labouring under any illusions, and the guys who want to fish can put food on the table and pay their crew. At least then we can have an industry where people aren't looking over their shoulders all the time. The alternative – continually thinning the quotas and squeezing fishermen until they're blue in the face – is painful and unnecessary for guys who work incredibly hard. Dinnae slash their throats and let them bleed to death.

A bit like Aberdeen, Peterhead has historically been very lucky. Aberdeen had a big fishing port for the whole of the nineteenth century and a good deal of the twentieth, too. The Aberdeen fish market used to be a hive of activity. Now the historic market building has been demolished, the fishing has declined and instead Aberdeen is the oil capital of Europe. In Peterhead, not only have we had fishing, but the oil rigs have helped to absorb some of the distress felt by the decline in the fleet.

But the oil won't last for ever. And then Peterhead might resemble its neighbouring town of Fraserburgh, which hasn't had the fortune of being near an off-shore oil industry. It depends one hundred per cent on the fishing, and it's facing a desperate battle for its future. It cannae afford to have its fishing wiped out.

The other places along the coastline – Banff, Buckie, Whitehills – had rich fishing traditions. Today, the industry's been completely wiped out in each of them. They're like ghost towns now. The number of communities that can rely on the fishing is getting smaller and smaller with every passing day.

I'm a self-made man. I got where I am today through hard work, a never-say-die spirit, and the occasional bit of gallows humour when things maybe weren't so sunny. To me, the most important thing in the world was getting ahead in life. I didn't want to be second best or on the giro, sipping from a bottle of Buckfast in the town centre.

But would I have been able to make a career for myself if I was starting out now? I'm not so sure. In my thirty-five-year career at sea, I have never seen morale so low as it is now. It sometimes seems like there's no hope. What hope could we possibly have if, three months before the end of the year, the quotas are almost exhausted, and those same quotas are to be slashed next year? If a fisherman can't make a living and a pay for his crew on 180 days a year at sea, how's he going to do it on 160 days? In fact I hear some fishing vessels may be cut to 100 days per year. No business can survive on that model.

Nobody's immune to the pressures. Prior to my foray into politics in the 2010 general election, as Conservative candidate for Banff & Buchan, the thought did cross my mind, albeit fleetingly, of taking a less active role in the fleet. I still have a lot to contribute and retirement hadn't figured in my thoughts. It was more of a quiet little voice chipping away at the back of my head. I like everything about the fishing; I love it. But fishing has had its heart torn out, and the industry's not the fun place it used to be. With all the rules and regulations, red tape and bureaucracy, it's no exaggeration to say a tagged prisoner has more basic freedom than the average skipper.

Not long ago I happened to be chatting with Andrew Buchan, another skipper in the fleet who was constructing a new vessel over in Macduff, the shipyard where I collected the *Amity II* from. Amid the excitement of taking command of the *Favonious*, we got on to the subject of a skipper's workload, and how it has changed since the mid-1980s. Back then my thoughts were totally focused on the business of catching fish.

Nowadays I need to juggle a number of demands: quotas, days at sea, day-to-day duties. None of these tasks is enjoyable, and they suck the energy out of the job.

We live in an authoritarian environment these days, where fishermen aren't trusted. If my satellite monitoring system breaks down at sea, I'm required to radio in to port once every four hours with an updated position. Before I can even put a single fish ashore, I've got to hand in my catch log-sheet – it's an offence if I don't. The log-sheet is a declaration of the catch you have on board. Should I swing so much as one box onto the quay without the log-sheet, I'd be looking at a court case.

If I'm approaching Peterhead and I've got more than a ton of cod on the *Amity II*, I've got to give the authorities four hours' warning before I come in to land, otherwise I'm not allowed to enter port. In spite of my years of experience, I find it difficult to keep up with the constant stream of rules imposed upon us; I cannot imagine how much of a struggle it is for a new skipper to remember everything.

I'm not going to sit back and be silent about this. The fishing has been good to me. It provided for my wonderful family, and opened up a lifestyle that was beyond my parents' reach.

The alternative to a healthy domestic fishery is a situation where we become a nation of importers instead of exporters. In Britain, we export eighty per cent of what we catch, and import eighty per cent of the fish we eat. That's a crazy statistic. Where's the logic and self-sufficiency in that? There's a human, community aspect to the fishing that sometimes gets lost amid the politics and bickering, and it's something I've come to appreciate in my town, where the industry and the people share a unique bond.

And it's a bond worth saving. In my time at sea, I've had the pleasure of fishing with some of the best skippers in the world, and I don't say that lightly. These are guys of real talent and skill, who've perfected their trade over many years of sailing. And we're in real danger of losing their expertise: without a steady flow of up-and-coming lads wanting to be a first mate or skipper, who are they supposed to pass their knowledge on to? The skills I'm talking about can't be taught by someone standing in front of a classroom.

Skippers are a breed apart. We're hunters in a modern world that is full of consumers but hardly any producers. And we can't teach the hunter instinct to people by giving a PowerPoint presentation to a generation of kids who are used to video games and digital TV.

Freedom's a big thing for a skipper. His ability to do his job depends on being able to pick and choose where he wants to fish, and what species he's hunting. That's how the fleet went from strength to strength in the past. Men like myself put our necks on the line, relying on gut instinct and experience to seek out and develop new fisheries.

My career has been a successful one because I was part of a producer organisation that had access to all types of fish on the east and west coasts of Scotland. I only ventured out to the west coast a couple of times and they weren't good trips, I didn't know the areas and the bountiful grounds. But at least I had the freedom to give it a go. Freedom of movement meant that I could go and fish where I reckoned was best for me. And without the crippling restrictions that are now imposed on us, we managed to turn the shellfish from a niche market into a mainstream one. It's that kind of ingenuity that's being dragged from under our feet.

At least I had the means and the ability to change up. My PO (Production Organisation) had access to the prawn quota, and the more generous quota numbers and days at sea meant I could afford to take a risk in switching to the prawns. Ten years after I took that decision, I'm effectively locked into it. That's all well and good if the sea stays exactly the same for the next fifty or a hundred years. But we know for a fact that it's chaos in the deep of the North Sea; what's top dog today is the loser tomorrow. Freddie the prawn's not going to be lording it for ever, and when that day arrives, all the skippers shut in to langoustine fishing will wake up to find their quotas not worth the pieces of paper they're printed on. Worse, the years of expertise in just one field means they'll be ill-equipped to start afresh in a totally new fishery. Instead of breeding 'fishermen', this generation is going into specific jobs. We might as well call them 'prawn men' or 'cod men' instead. The bottom line is, if the North Sea filled up overnight with whitefish, a guy like me would be bankrupt.

British people have a longstanding relationship with the sea and the health of the merchant navy matters to them. That's why it's vital we be honest with ourselves about the current state of the fishing: so we'll properly address the problems facing us, rather than burying our heads in the sand and pretending everything's hunky dory.

There are, though, reasons to be optimistic about the industry's future, despite the current state of affairs. Following the success of *Trawlermen*, the training course for new entrants in Fraserburgh became oversubscribed, at a time when people feared the course might have to be discontinued, as so few guys went in for the certificate. If we can get young people interested in the fishing as a viable career, we'll have half a chance of maintaining a strong fleet.

And there's the current batch of young skippers, guys like James West, Charles Bruce and many more like them. They see opportunity and challenges, where perhaps older fishermen can't. My good friend James is a guy who you look at and think, 'Brilliant skipper.' The scary thing about James is that he's only in his early thirties and he's already achieved so much. He comes from a rich fishing dynasty, and he's also got two younger brothers, Robert and Andrew, in the industry. Robert has now gone on to skipper his own vessel, while James and Andrew took delivery of a brand new state-of-the-art trawler in September 2010. James will continue to have a fantastic career, simply because he's forward-thinking. As everyone else is bailing out, he's putting his money where his mouth is; a shrewd approach, because if the fishing does enter a boom period again, he'll be in an excellent position, with a new boat, steady crew and the experience to make it work. Good times lie ahead for James and his team.

Back in the 1980s, when the fishing was enduring a turbulent time, James's father commissioned a new boat. The timing seemed awful. Older skippers looked at his supposed folly and muttered under their breath, 'Wouldn't like to be James West building at a time like this.' But James made it work, and his son, I'm sure, will do the same.

Charles Bruce, another young skipper with real quality, framed it best when he said, 'Fifty years ago my father said the fishing was finished. But we're still gaun today. There'll be fishing as long as there's fish in the sea.'

Too right. The fishing doesn't end. It's been in the doldrums before and survived, and sometimes flourished. However, when it emerges from a bad period, it undergoes change. And sometimes that change is painful. The big question is, what will the industry look like in twenty years? How will the North Sea look, and which species will be king of the food chain then? Nobody knows. But I hope that in decades to come, Peterhead keeps up its proud tradition of sending hunters to the sea.

13

THE SECRET LIFE OF THE SEA

If the *Amity II* is my second home, then the North Sea is my office.

Early on in my career, I decided that if I wanted to be a successful trawlerman, I had to make it my business to know every contour and valley in that vast body of water. The North Sea is some six hundred miles long and three hundred and fifty miles wide, stretching from the Dover Straits and the English Channel all the way up to the Norwegian Sea, connecting it to the Atlantic Ocean. There's 300,000 square miles of fishing ground, and I had to know the lot of it like the back of my hand.

People take the seabed to be a calm, flat landscape, but the reality is very different. It's a violent, bumpy, chaotic place. If you want to have an idea of how the bottom of the sea appears, go out and look at the countryside. The terrain would look the same underwater too. Inclines would be ridges created by movements along the continental shelf, tectonic plates knocking into each other, and the steep edges of the hills would be awash with lovely prawns hiding from monkfish beneath stones and rocks. Grassy embankments would be brimming with haddock and cod shoals in the evening, when they come out to feed.

This is my hunting ground.

The North Sea has a long heritage as a good fishing source, dating back for centuries. In the early 1960s, skippers from north-east Scotland were considered pioneers of the fishing grounds as more powerful and modern boats allowed them to fish ever further from home. Some even left a legacy behind them. Dotted around the North Sea are pieces of ground named after various fishermen who pioneered trips to those areas and came back with good returns. One piece is called Willie Buck's Shoal, in honour of an old Peterhead skipper named William Buchan (no relation to me, but he was James West's grandfather). Another skipper by the name of Adam Stewart also has a shoal named after him two hundred miles to the north of the port. To date no bit of sea has been honoured with the Jimmy Buchan name, but I'm hoping it's just a matter of time!

One of my favourite fishing grounds is the Devil's Hole, one of the deepest areas of the North Sea. This is one of a group of about five deep ravines or trenches. Each one runs in a north–south direction for about fifteen miles, reaching as deep as 750 feet below the water surface in places. The other trenches all have names too, like the Pair o' Pants and the Ouse Hole. I've no idea where those names come from, but the Devil's Hole definitely didn't get its name for nothing. Filled with rocks and mud holes housing prize-catch langoustine, the hole is also littered with massive boulders weighing several tons, which will tear your nets to shreds should you snag one. Because the trenches are very narrow, in places just a mile wide, and have steep sides, trawler nets can easily get caught, putting a boat in serious trouble. A torn net can cost thousands of pounds to repair if the damage is extensive.

For a skipper it's not enough to simply go to areas that have yielded big catches in the past. Fish move in cycles, and an area of the sea that provided you with a bumper return one year might give you a haul of nothing but mud and rocks the next. To run a successful boat, you have to develop a deep under-standing of the habits of the fish you're catching. There are a lot of different terrains out there under the North Sea: sandy bottoms, muddy bottoms, stony bottoms; and it can be very hard sometimes for the skipper to find the right location to make a good haul.

The North Sea is prone to getting battered by extreme weather. There have been some incredibly harsh winters. One year I was listening to the shipping forecast and heard the out-look for the last sea area, Southeast Iceland. It's always the last because it is the furthest fishing ground from the UK. It was a bitterly cold January morning and I couldn't feel my fingers or my toes, but the weather off the coast of Iceland sounded like it was a great deal worse. *Moderate icing*, the forecaster announced. That would mean any nearby boats would probably ice up.

I'd experienced light icing a few times during my berth on the *Fidelia*. The rails, mast, aerials, everything was frozen. The waters thrown over the boat would also freeze, creating a layer of ice on every surface, and a rail that was an inch thick would suddenly be three inches. The stability of the boat was affected and moving about on the deck was impossible as it had been turned into an ice-rink. The winds were freezing and, beneath my boots, my toes were just about dropping off. For two days we had to slip and slide around the boat, clinging on for dear life, gulping down cups of tea and hot soups to keep ourselves warm. Finally, on the third day, the temperature lifted a little, and the icing started to melt.

I hated the winters. You would have to wear thick layers of clothes just to keep yourself from freezing to death. I'd turn up at the harbour for work wearing thick socks, simmets (a type of vest), a shirt, woollen jumper, duffel coat, the lot. I was wearing so many layers I could hardly move around!

However wretched the winters were, the fog was worse. Fog could be an absolute horror to get through and was a fairly regular occurrence in the months of April, May and June in and around the North Sea; hot air coming up from the

Continent would mix with cold air from the north, a first-class recipe for creating fog. Even with all the modern navigation systems, a skipper still needs to see where he's going. If you can't see, whether you have ten satellite systems and radars or one, you are still navigating blind. On one particular trip, the fog was so thick that you could cut it up and package it. I was standing up in the wheelhouse and yet I couldn't see the front of the boat. It was a very eerie, disorientating atmosphere, the sea quiet as an ice cap. All I could hear was the faintest soft lapping of the waves. Steering through that felt like driving through a cloud thirty miles long.

The fog isn't just spooky; it disorientates. I had literally no idea where I was in relation to other shipping. I had a plotter that told me my position and a compass to tell my heading, but if those suddenly failed, we'd be lost with no clear way of getting home. I stepped out of the wheelhouse. A dirty grey, wet, cold mist encircled the boat like a smoke ring, the fog lying flat on the surface of the sea. I couldn't see anything in front of me, but when I looked above, I did a double-take. I saw a clear blue sky and, incredibly, a shining sun. Utterly surreal. I didn't stay on the deck for long. In such impenetrable fog, the only way I could avoid a fatal collision was to keep a constant eye on the radar, picking up other boats. The radar was no guarantee, however. Small boats are difficult to pick up on the radar and if a skipper didn't keep a close tab on the screen he could easily miss one.

Returning to harbour in foggy weather was also laced with

danger. It was common to have all the crew gathered together on the whaleback, looking for the breakwaters to help steer the boat safely back into port. The skip would be navigating in, lining up the channel into the harbour, with the crew up on deck listening for the fog horn as well. When the fog finally cleared, everyone would breathe a sigh of relief; I, for one, was always thankful when it passed with my boat still intact. There were times when the fog would last an entire week; your eyes would be sore looking into the radar for targets. Those occasions were absolute misery, the pits.

At other times the North Sea was more like the Sahara. During the summers the sun would beat down on us from a cloudless blue dome, and I'd be sitting out on the deck in my trunks sunbathing. Summers were really hot, just as winters were painfully cold. In the last few years, that hasn't really been the case. Summers at sea now are grey, dark and dank, and in winter you never hear 'moderate or light icing' coming over the shipping forecast any more, not even in Southeast Iceland. Seasonality has shifted, with more angry depressions coming through compared with twenty years ago.

As for me, well, I turned fifty still in the role of skipper. I've remained in the fishing through thick and thin because, to a certain degree, it's a good way of life. The fishing is also hard, because of the harsh environment I've spent most of my adult life in. But there are benefits. I get more time at home than I used to as a young lad, when I'd be working six days a week, every week of the year. Now I get three or four days' grace between trips, and sometimes up to a week, if the weather's bad. Because quotas limit the number of days I can spend at sea on the *Amity II*, I pay close attention to the weather reports. Whereas in the past I would've set sail in a northerly gale, now I have to balance the need to go to sea with the reality that I'd spend most of the first or second day riding a storm. When I read reports of incoming gales on the eve of a trip today, I'll usually take a commercial decision to stay at home for an extra night. Storms may make for dramatic viewing on primetime television, but they don't exactly aid a skipper in his bid to land a big catch.

There is a downside to spending a night in a warm bed and having dinner with your loved ones. Simply, you're not producing any fish for the markets, and without any fish, you can't make any money.

I have a ferocious work ethic; all skippers do. We work hard, because the share system means fishermen only get rewarded for producing. If we dinnae produce, we dinnae get a pay.

The traditional view is that fishermen are a greedy bunch. People read the papers and think, 'They want to catch more and more fish ... they won't stop until they've drained the sea of every living thing.' But that's not true. We're just guys trying to make a living and provide for our families. One single trip sometimes has to last us for three or four weeks, when the weather is bad or the vessel is broken down, and then there's all the times we don't get paid: not only the days at home between trips, but the Christmas period, when the fish market dries up and the fleet's vessels are tied up at port for their annual refits. When we do sail we're at the mercy of the sea. If the weather's stormy or the catches for some reason are poor, our profits go through the floor. In our industry, no fish equals no pay.

You might ask, 'What motivates skippers to get up and work each day, if things are as bad as you say?' My answer to that is, we live for the moments when our uncommon lifestyle pays off. At Christmas every fisherman gets a proper holiday. I understand that people with desk jobs have to work over the holidays, whereas I'm able to put up my feet from the twenty-first of December until early January, spend some quality time with my family and friends and generally relax. A proper break makes the job easier – as does having a good crew, and I've been lucky to work with guys like Geoff and Kevin, people I consider my friends. The job is what you make it, and as a skipper it's up to you to decide what kind of a crew you want, and what sort of a boat. When I did manage to assemble a good crew, I nurtured it, and the friendships I struck up with the other guys became very special, because of the close conditions we inhabited, and the dramas we shared.

Sometimes I'll be at sea, drinking in the fresh air on a mild day when the gales and winds are a distant memory, and I think to myself, I wouldn't swap this job for any other. The hours may be long and the work strenuous, but few jobs in the world give you the opportunity to work as a hunter, pitting your wits against Mother Nature.

The future holds uncertainty for us. However, I think it also holds change – and change can be exciting as well as worrying. History shows us that what fishermen were doing twenty or thirty years ago was different to what we're engaged in today. Another twenty years down the line, it'll shift yet again.

I often wonder to myself, what will the North Sea look like in 2030? Maybe squid or hake will have become the predominant species by that date. These are stocks that, in my opinion, are on the cusp of becoming abundant in the North Sea. Hake is a weird one, but it just might go on to conquer the food chain. Its normal breeding grounds are the deep waters of the Mediterranean and the Atlantic Ocean and it's a big dish in Spanish and Portuguese cuisine.

My colleagues and I are now seeing hake catches in increasing numbers. Hake, like cod before it, is a predator. It'll eat anything and it's no surprise that it's begun muscling in around our neck of the woods. As things stand, the European Commission disagrees about the level of hake in the North Sea, so we fishermen aren't able to get a sizeable quota catching it. In the meantime, the hake's got a free run at chomping its way up the food chain. That's my theory, anyway.

Suppose the hake drives the cod out of the water. What then? It's impossible to predict what will happen. But whatever the future holds, I hope that Peterhead still has its close connection to the sea, and its sons and brothers are still going out to hunt the big prizes.

One thing I can say for sure is, I won't be at sea in five years' time. Once I turned fifty, I knew that the clock was ticking and I'd soon have to call time on my career. In fact, I promised Irene that I'd stop the fishing when I hit forty – but I never really had any intention of sticking to that one!

In the wider scheme of things, fifty's not old, but it is for the job of running a boat. Skippering is a young man's game. You get to the point where trips take it out of you physically, and you start to lose a little bit of your edge. Once that happens, you know deep down that it's time to think about hanging up your oilskins. It's not something that a skipper decides overnight, but after a while he has to face up to the fact that he belongs ashore.

When I do finally step off the *Amity II* for the last time, I'll do so with a lifetime of memories to treasure and a twinge of sadness in my heart. It's only natural to feel a sense of loss when something you've done for most of your life comes to an end. As the saying goes, the boat is more than a boat. My heart won't be heavy, though, and I intend to look forward to a new chapter in my career.

Fishermen need all the help they can get. They have their families and friends; they have the Missions; they have, too, the support and good wishes of millions of people across the country, thanks to the BBC.

I've been a fisherman all my adult life, and a skipper for a great deal of that. I know what it's like to juggle the pressures of running a business and supporting a family. I'm used to working in confined spaces and building up relationships with people. I've learnt to respect the sea and navigate through storms. And I've seen how decision-making and red tape have combined to make a skipper's job fiendishly hard. All these experiences have stood me in good stead on the boat, and I believe they'll come in handy when I focus my attention on shore.

Trawlermen has been a wonderful thing in terms of promoting the fishing. But it doesn't really show the private tensions that tap away at a skipper's mind. The fear of losing his livelihood and his home. The constant dark cloud hovering over his head, the voice that wonders, Will I make it next year? People are talking about cuts to this or that service in a time of recession; well, I've known nothing but cuts in twenty years of skippering a vessel. We didn't have any choice except to knuckle down and get on with it.

Fishing has taught me valuable lessons about life. We're creatures of habit, and we tend to resent change, anything that upsets the status quo. Yet at the same time, change is what gives us a boost when we're stuck in a rut and feeling sorry for ourselves. Whether it's a new food chain in the North Sea or a shift in attitudes towards quotas, or even technology creating whole new types of fishing, things will look quite different tomorrow.

The one thing that won't change is the skipper. He'll still be out there, riding the rough waves, poring over maps in his wheelhouse, sniffing out the fish.

I'm proud to say I've been a Peterhead fisherman. There's

no one else in Britain like us, which probably explains why we're such a close-knit group of people. We've been through good times and bad, celebrated big catches and felt the pain at the loss of a friend in stormy weather. Through it all we've stuck together, as a family, a crew, a fleet and a community. That's ultimately why I hope the fishing thrives in the Blue Toon: it's given us everything we hold dear to us today. Whether it's aboard the *Amity II*, fundraising for the Fishermen's Mission or speaking out for the plight of the industry, I'll continue giving back to a life and a career that's provided me with friendships and memories, love and success.